basic

ISLINGTON

West Library
Bridgeman Road
London N1 1BD
Tel: 020 7527 7920

R

Library & Cultural Services

This item should be returned on or before the last date stamped below.
Users who do not return items promptly may be liable to overdue charges.
When renewing items please quote the number on your membership card.

Lib.1

Hodder Murray

A MEMBER OF THE HODDER HEADLINE GROUP

Other titles in this series:

Basic Punctuation   Don Shiach   ISBN   0 7195 7027 1
Basic Spelling   Michael Temple   ISBN   0 7195 7026 3
Basic Written English Don Shiach   ISBN   0 7195 7030 1

© Don Shiach 1995
First published 1995 by
Hodder Murray, a member of the Hodder Headline Group
338 Euston Road
London NW1 3BH

Reprinted 1997, 1998, 1999. 2002, 2003, 2004 (twice), 2005, 2006

Layouts by Ann Samuel
Typeset by Servis Filmsetting Ltd, Longsight, Manchester
Printed and bound in Malta

A CIP record for this book is available from the British Library.

ISBN-10: 0 7195 7028 X
ISBN-13: 978 0 7195 7028 5

CONTENTS

INTRODUCTION

WHAT WILL THIS BOOK DO FOR ME?

- Grammar is the system people use to communicate effectively. It allows us to organise words into a pattern that makes sense.
    A better understanding of grammar helps us to express ourselves more clearly and effectively.
- A better understanding of our language helps us to make a good impression when it is important to do so. For example when we are:
    - in an exam
    - in a job interview
    - returning a faulty item to a shop
    - filling in forms
    - making a presentation
    - making arrangements by telephone
    - writing letters.
- If the language we use is not clear, then people may not make the effort to understand what we are saying.
- Understanding grammatical rules and applying them to speaking and writing English can help you to present yourself to the rest of the world.
- In these situations, people who are familiar with the rules of grammar are at an advantage.

HOW WILL THIS BOOK HELP ME?

- This book will help you to identify types of words. It will tell you, or remind you, of the existence of certain categories of words called **parts of speech**:

nouns	pronouns	adjectives	adverbs	prepositions	conjunctions
		articles	interjections		

- Recognising these types of words gives you the tools to describe language and to understand how it works. With these tools, you will be better equipped to use the language.
- You also need to know how to use these basic categories of words in **sentences**. Just as there are various types of words, there are various types of sentences. This book will help you to construct sentences correctly and appropriately.

- The first thing you should do is to use the **Self-assessment questionnaire** on page 5 to check your own strengths and weaknesses. Then you can concentrate on those areas where you need most practice.

PUTTING IT INTO PRACTICE

- The aim of mastering the grammar of any language is to be able to speak and write that language expertly and clearly. In this book, you will be given plenty of opportunities in the structured **Checkpoints** to use the grammatical terms and rules you have learnt and to check that you are using them appropriately by consulting the answers given at the back of the book.
- Making the transfer between acquiring knowledge and putting it into practice is the crucial test for any new skill. Learning grammatical terms and rules is pointless unless you are able to apply them. In the **Activities** you will have the chance to apply what you have learnt in realistic contexts.
- As you work your way through this book, make sure you look out for opportunities in everyday life to use what you have learnt in order to **say and write what you really mean**. That is the point of grammar.

WHAT IS GRAMMAR AND WHY DOES IT MATTER?

- Grammar is the set of rules that describes how language works. English grammar describes how English works.
- Grammar describes the relationship between different types of words, and the way those words behave and change when they are used in different ways.

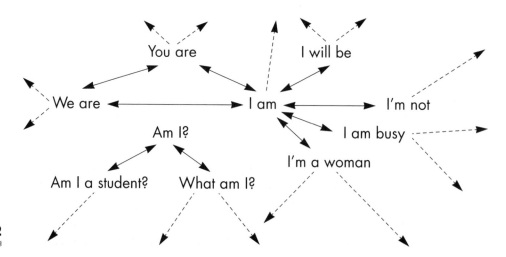

In this diagram each arrow represents how one grammatical rule changes the words we use.

'Am' changes to 'are' when it comes after 'we'.

If 'I' and 'am' swap places they make a question.

- Like any topic, grammar has its own vocabulary to describe and discuss it.

  It is possible to speak English without knowing the difference between a noun and a pronoun, or being able to describe how a sentence is structured. If you want to improve your English, however, familiarity with these terms will actually make the grammar **easier**.

- Grammatical terms are precise definitions. If, in a DIY shop, you wanted to buy some of the straight, metal, sharpish things with smooth sides, rather than the ones with a spiral groove running from the flat end to the point, it would be much simpler if you knew the words for 'nail' and 'screw'.

- In grammar, if you know the words then you can **understand your mistakes** in general terms, and you can be given clear guidelines to avoid making them.

- If you learn the grammatical terms you will also discover how much grammar you already know, without even being aware of it. You already use this knowledge to create everything you say or write.

HOW DO WE BEGIN TO LEARN GRAMMAR?

- As very young children, we learn, without being conscious of it, the basic patterns of language. We listen to older people and we imitate their patterns of speech.

  Mostly, we begin by getting things wrong. Children put words in the wrong order and in the wrong grammatical relationship with one another:

  Me Mummy want.

  Him work.

  Gradually we learn the patterns of word order and grammatical forms, but we learn from what we hear, so it is possible to pick up incorrect patterns as well as appropriate ones.

STANDARD ENGLISH AND EVERYDAY LANGUAGE

- Standard English means the type of English that is conventionally used in education, in business, in the media and most written communications, and in most other contexts that are 'public' rather than 'private'.

- This usually sounds more formal than the type of English we use in communicating with our friends, family and local community. Most of us,

3

for example, are familiar with a dialect of English which has, to a certain extent, its own separate vocabulary and set of grammatical rules. It is not the case that Standard English has grammar and our own everyday English does not; remember that grammar **describes** every use of language. It is also not the case that Standard English has to sound pompous and fussy. It is meant to be an aid to clear communication, not an obstacle.

Consider these examples:

We was only playing a friendly.

I'm no going there tonight.

Both these statements might be quite appropriate in the context of an informal situation amongst people familiar with these 'dialect' features (remember, a dialect is a version of a language shared by some, but not all, speakers of that language). They would, however, be considered 'incorrect' in terms of Standard English.

- You need a knowledge of the grammar of Standard English for situations when you need to communicate clearly with people whose everyday English may not be the same as yours.

 When you want to create a favourable impression, and leave no room for doubt as to what you mean, applying the rules of Standard English enables you to reach a wider audience than if you use grammar that might be appropriate in much more informal situations, such as when you are with family and friends.

- Improving your grammar can be fun and will broaden your horizons. There will be many occasions in life where it will be to your advantage to use Standard English correctly and clearly.

SELF-ASSESSMENT QUESTIONNAIRE

It is likely that you will need to concentrate on particular parts of this book depending on your strengths and weaknesses. This questionnaire is designed to help you to assess your present knowledge. Answer the questions, then check your answers against those given on page 103. Add up the number of marks you have earned in each section and check what your performance means in terms of the degree of help you need.

NOUNS

1 Read the following letter and write down 11 **nouns** that are used in it. Do not choose more than 11 words.

> Dear Kate,
>   The weather here has been truly awful. Not one hot day so far! Why come on holiday at all, I ask myself, when it's like this.
>   My parents complain all the time about the hotel. The food is only so-so and the beach is not very sandy.
>   Oh, well, it'll soon be over. See you next week. Yours etc. Rose.

2 Read this newspaper report about a motorway accident. Write down 26 separate **common nouns** that are used in the report.

COACH IN HORRIFIC M1 ACCIDENT

A party of old age pensioners was involved in a multiple accident on a busy motorway yesterday. Three people were killed and ten retained in the nearby Royal Hospital for observation. The accident occurred on the M1 near the junction with the M6 when the coach carrying the pensioners on an outing to the seaside was involved in a collision with a lorry and several cars.

A fire started on the coach and passengers had to leave by the emergency hatch. The driver of the lorry was rushed to hospital with serious injuries.

'It's too early to determine the cause of this tragedy,' said the police officer in charge of the unit that rushed to the scene of the accident, 'but the vehicle was travelling in the fast lane when it hit the van.'

3 Pick out eight **abstract nouns** that are used in this conversation between television experts commenting on a football match. Restrict your choice to eight different words, ignore repetitions.

PRESENTER It just goes to show you, it's a funny old world.
EXPERT It certainly is. But when all's said and done, it's all about winning.
PRESENTER You can say that again.
EXPERT When all's said and done, it's all about . . .
PRESENTER No, no, I didn't mean that literally. What else is it about?
EXPERT It's about courage and tenacity.
PRESENTER And skill. Let's not forget skill.
EXPERT And the will to win.
PRESENTER Yes, let's not forget hunger for success.
EXPERT And the honour of winning, let's not forget that.
PRESENTER When all's said and done.
EXPERT Exactly!

Assess what you know about nouns by turning to the answers on page 103. Award yourself a mark for every correct answer and then check what your performance means in terms of the degree of help you need.

Score more than 40 out of 45: you seem to have no difficulty with nouns!
Score between 25 and 40: you need to brush up on some points about nouns; see Section 2.
Score less than 25: your knowledge of nouns is fairly limited; pay very close attention to the explanations and activities in Section 2.

VERBS

1 Read the following advertisement for a brand of trainers. There are 26 **verbs** used in the advert. Make a list of them, restricting yourself to 26 choices in all (including repeated words and verbs made up of more than one word).

Want the **best** trainers in the world?

Are you willing to pay that bit extra?

○ Of course, there are trainers that you can buy cheaper than **TIKE** trainers. We know that, but it doesn't worry us. Cheap imitators never do.

○ Because here at **TIKE** we pride ourselves on making the best trainers in the world. What makes us think so? Top athletes tell us we do. Millions of satisfied customers across the world write to us. Top-class stores rate us the tops.

○ But our kind of excellence doesn't come cheap. So, if you think small, or are a bit of a cheapskate, don't buy **TIKE**, go for the competition.

○ But it will show. Are you good enough for **TIKE**? Do you consider you deserve **TIKE**? Well then, what's stopping you? On your starting blocks . . .

2 Subject–verb agreements.

Read the following advice leaflet. For each gap you are given a choice of verb forms. Write down the form that is correct in each gap.

If you .... long-term unemployed ...	is/are
Everybody .... a job. But hunting for employment .... time and know-how. The government and local employers .... co-operated to set up a service to help people who .... been unemployed for over six months.	want/wants take/takes has/have has/have
The services we .... access to word-processors and the supply of materials. There .... also skilled advisers on hand to give advice on presentation.	provide/provides include/includes is/are
Anybody over 18 who .... been unemployed for six months or longer can take advantage of this service. Each of the centres .... situated centrally. Everybody .... treated the same and a friendly welcome .... guaranteed.	has/have is/are is/are is/are
Applications .... not required. Each of our centres .... open between 10 a.m. and 6 p.m. Monday to Friday. Practical help and advice .... at hand.	is/are is/are is/are
Good news .... always welcome, so .... your friends about us.	is/are tell/tells

Assess what you know about verbs by checking your answers on page 103. Award one mark for every correct answer. Then check the total marks you are awarded against the advice given below.

Score more than 38 out of 43: you know your verbs very well.
Score between 24 and 38: look carefully at Section 3.
Score less than 24: your knowledge of verbs is limited; work your way through Section 3 very carefully.

SENTENCES

1 Read the dialogue below. It is divided into numbered sections. Write down two headings: *Complete sentences* and *Incomplete sentences*. Decide which sections of the dialogue are in the form of a complete sentence and which are in the form of an incomplete sentence.

BOB   (1) Why didn't you go?
ROSE (2) Because it was too hot.
BOB   (3) But a cricket match is nice when it's hot. (4) Not boiling, of course. (5) But warm.
ROSE (6) Well, maybe. (7) I went to a film instead.
BOB   (8) To a film in that hot weather? (9) Why?
ROSE (10) Because the cinema was air-conditioned. (11) And, anyway, Mel Bigson.
BOB   (12) Mel Bigson? (13) Who's he?
ROSE (14) Honestly (15) A movie star. (16) Come off it! (17) Having me on like that! (17)
BOB   (18) I'd prefer a cricket match to Mel Bigson any day.

2 Below is an extract from a speech by a politician. Write down the subject of each underlined verb.

'My party <u>does not make</u> empty promises as our opponents <u>do</u>. Winning your vote through raising false hopes <u>is</u> not a game we <u>play</u>. If voters <u>do not trust</u> us, then our prospects as a government <u>are</u> dismal. For example, we frankly <u>admit</u> that taxes <u>may have to be</u> increased in the future. Schools, hospitals, benefits and defence all <u>have to be paid for</u>. Anyone with any kind of intelligence <u>knows</u> that money <u>does not grow</u> on trees. That <u>is</u> what the other lot <u>think</u>, not us. We <u>know</u> that every advance we <u>make</u> <u>has to be earned</u> by hard work. We <u>know</u> that improvements in education and health care <u>have to be paid for</u>. We <u>know</u> that people <u>are willing to pay</u> higher taxes if they <u>can see</u> that the money <u>is being used</u> to help those in need. No, my friends, I <u>will leave</u> the false promises to my opponents. Because the electorate <u>is</u> intelligent and not foolish, my party <u>will form</u> the next government of this country.'

Assess what you know about sentences by checking your answers on page 103. Count up your marks and check your total against the advice given below.

   Score more than 39 out of 42: you have no problems with sentences.
   Score between 22 and 39: look carefully at Sections 3 and 8.
   Score between 15 and 24: you need to work on this area. Work your way through Sections 3 and 8.

ADJECTIVES AND ADVERBS

Read the article below about the Hollywood film industry. 23 adjectives and eight adverbs are used in the article. Make two lists under the headings *Adjectives* and *Adverbs*.

CONFIDENT HOLLYWOOD LOOKS FOR THE BIG BUCKS

Hollywood studios are banking on summer hits to boost their already bulging bank accounts. As the American long school vacation starts, hungry producers are waiting anxiously but enthusiastically for the new releases to hit the nation's cinemas.

Many movies are aimed cynically at the youth market. Ageing producers who clearly do not enjoy pop culture are eagerly pouring millions into teen films about young love, loveable pets and parents who get their comeuppance.

It's the popcorn-eating teenagers who make up the bulk of the huge audience that awaits popular hits. Literally billions of dollars can be made by astute film makers who hit the button accurately.

Assess what you know about adjectives and adverbs by checking your answers on page 103. Count up the marks for your correct answers and then check your total against the advice given below.

Score more than 28 out of 31: you have a very sound knowledge of adjectives and adverbs.

Score between 14 and 28: clearly you need some help with adjectives and adverbs and you should practise, using Sections 4 and 5.

Score less than 14: you need to work carefully through Sections 4 and 5.

1
N O U N S
D E F I N I N G   T H E   W O R L D

- **Nouns are the names of all the many things, places, feelings, thoughts, qualities, people and animals that make up our experience of the world.**
- **Nouns are used to differentiate one thing from another, one place from another, one person from another, and so on.**
- **Nouns, in other words, enable us to define the world around us.**
- **Without nouns, we would not be able to identify in one word the difference between, say, a dog and a cat, or between sadness and happiness, or a train and a ship.**
- **You need to be able to identify nouns so that you can use them appropriately to communicate clearly with other people in both speech and writing.**
- **The more nouns you know, the better equipped you will be to define your world.**

TYPES OF NOUNS

We can think of nouns as belonging to four main categories:

common nouns   abstract nouns   proper nouns   collective nouns

■ COMMON NOUNS

- **Common nouns** are, as you might deduce from their name, the most frequent type of noun.
- **Common nouns** name things:

SHOPPING LIST

✓coffee   ✓peas
✓tea   ✗wardrobe
✓baked beans   ✗chairs
✓socks   ✓sofa
✓kettle

LIST OF ITEMS
FOR SALE

1, A BOX OF RECORDS
2, TWO ARM CHAIRS
3, A SEWING MACHINE
4, A MUSIC CENTRE
5, A CARTON OF BOOKS
6, A TELEVISION SET

• **Common nouns** name living creatures:

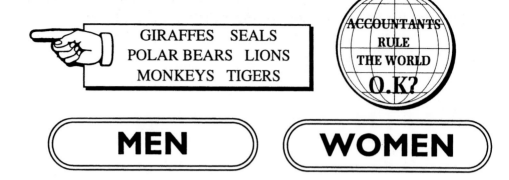

• **Common nouns** name places:

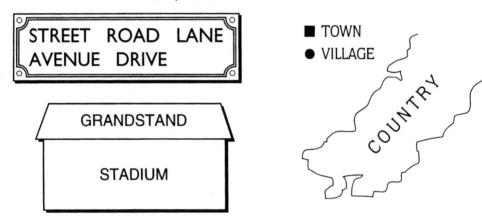

• **Common nouns** name types of people:

✓ *Checkpoint A*

Read through the following article and either circle or make a list of the common nouns that have been used. Other types of nouns have also been used; ignore these and list only the common nouns.

POP GROUP IN RIOT!

Guitars were smashed, windows broken and seats slashed as the fans of the pop group Get Lost went on rampage last night.

Get Lost ended their gig at the Dawley Centre by smashing seemingly expensive instruments.

Lead singer Max Firebrand, led the way. The fans seemed to go into an imitative frenzy as they attacked the hall and even some of the attendants.

'It has nothing to do with Get Lost,' said Firebrand later. 'We certainly did not want the venue damaged.'

A spokesman for the Dawley Centre said repairs would cost several thousand pounds.

■ ABSTRACT NOUNS

- **Abstract nouns** name anything that has no actual physical existence: feelings, qualities or ideas.
- Abstract nouns name **feelings** such as:
  helplessness   sorrow   anger   gratitude   betrayal
- Abstract nouns name **qualities** such as:
  reliability   courage   generosity   intelligence   stupidity
- Abstract nouns name **ideas** or **thoughts** such as:
  freedom   equality   friendship   slavery   dictatorship.

HERE'S YOUR ORDER OF NOUNS, MADAM.

I CAN SEE THE COMMON, PROPER AND COLLECTIVE NOUNS, BUT WHERE ARE MY ABSTRACTS?

YOU CAN'T SEE THEM, MADAM, BUT I ASSURE YOU THEY ARE THERE.

✓ *Checkpoint B*

Read the following extract from a speech. Circle or make a list of the abstract nouns that are used. Other types of nouns are used, but ignore these and select only the abstract nouns.

> *'Friends, ask yourselves this. Can any society give real equality to every citizen? Isn't that just a fantasy? We have to ask ourselves whether equality is even a worthwhile goal. I would argue that freedom of choice is much more important and the pursuit of equality is a useless dream. A nation thrives on the differences between people, not on their uniformity.'*

■ PROPER NOUNS

- **Proper nouns** are the actual names of particular people, places and things. 'Whitney Houston' names a particular person; 'Australia' names a particular place; 'Concorde' names a particuar thing.
- Proper nouns include the names of **towns**, **districts** and **villages**.

BUNTHORPE
Twinned With
Oberschlagen, Switzerland

BRIXTON

- Proper nouns include the names of **buildings**, **streets**, **mountains** and **rivers**.

THE NATIONAL GALLERY

NORTH STREET

RIVER DEE

- Proper nouns include the names of the **months** of the year, the **days** of the week, **festivals** and special occasions.

  January February March April May . . .
  Sunday Monday Tuesday Wednesday . . .
  Christmas Yom Kippur Ramadan . . .
  New Year's Day Hogmanay Easter . . .

- Proper nouns include the names of **organisations, institutions** and **brands**.

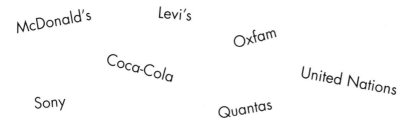

McDonald's   Levi's
                              Oxfam
          Coca-Cola
                                        United Nations
Sony
                    Quantas

- Proper nouns include the names of particular **people**.

  Steffi Graf   Brian Lara   Michelle Pfeiffer

- Proper nouns include the names of **books**, **films** and **songs** etc.

- All **proper nouns** start with a **capital letter**. If there are two or more words in the name, both or all the words have to have capital letters, (except small words such as of, and, the, in, etc.).

  the Bank of Scotland   the White House

✓ Checkpoint C

Read the following magazine article about Elvis Presley. Circle or make a list of the proper nouns that are used. Ignore any other type of noun.

Elvis Presley was born in Tennessee in the United States in 1935. He died in Memphis in 1977. In his comparatively short lifetime, Presley recorded some of the most famous rock 'n' roll records of all time: 'Heartbreak Hotel', 'Blue Suede Shoes', 'Hound Dog', 'Love Me Tender' and 'Jailhouse Rock'.

Elvis was known as 'The King' and he is still adored by millions of fans across the world. In Japan, thousands of collectors will buy any item of memorabilia associated with Elvis; in France there are legions of fans and in Great Britain, followers of the 'One-and-Only' meet regularly to worship at the shrine.

■ COLLECTIVE NOUNS

Collective nouns are the names given to groups of people, animals or things which are regarded as **a whole**.

herd flock crop team

a fleet of ships   a collection of dolls   a gaggle of geese

✓ *Checkpoint D*

1   Read the following article from a local newspaper. Circle or make a list of all the collective nouns that have been used. Ignore any other type of noun.

BIKERS CAUSE NO DAMAGE!

Yesterday around midday, a very large group of motor-bike riders rode onto the seafront at Beachpool. Holiday-makers stood and watched as the swarm of bikers seemed to take over the area like a well-trained army. The police were alerted immediately.

'I think the community expected trouble,' said a police spokesperson. 'But what happened was the gang bought ice-creams and departed as peaceably as they had arrived.'

'People have the wrong idea of bikers,' said one bearded rider. 'We all belong to a club and all we're interested in is moving on, man.'

1 Gaps have been left in the following passages. Fill each with a noun of the type indicated in square brackets, choosing one that makes sense in the context.

  a) The [abstract noun] of drugs in [abstract noun] is an ever-present [abstract noun]. Famous sports stars such as [proper noun] have had their [abstract noun] ruined by taking [common noun]. The [abstract noun] is what the [common noun] can do to eradicate this [abstract noun].

  b) 'Secret Weapon III' is a superb [common noun]. Its [collective noun] of stars, [proper noun] and [proper noun], are adored by [common noun] and the [common noun] is bound to be a [abstract noun]. The [abstract noun] of the film is the usual mixture of [common noun] and [abstract noun]. The action is set in [proper noun] and the [abstract noun] never lets up. Go to your nearest [common noun] and do yourself a [abstract noun].

2 a) Write a mini-story (no more than 100 words long) with the title 'The Special Meal'. When you use nouns in this story, use only common nouns.

  b) Write a mini-story (again no longer than 100 words) with the title 'My Hero' or 'My Heroine'. You may use up to five **common nouns**; the rest of the nouns you use must be **abstract nouns**.

'THE', 'A' OR 'AN'?

- Very often, the **definite** or **indefinite article** comes in front of a noun.
- The definite article is the word '**the**'.
- It is called the **definite** article because by using 'the' a **particular** person, thing or feeling is indicated: the woman, the train, the book.
- The indefinite article is the word '**a**' or '**an**'.
- It is called the **indefinite** article because it does not indicate any particular person, thing or feeling. It refers to the **general**: a woman, a train, a book.
- 'The', the definite article, can be both singular and plural: the women, the trains, the books.
- 'A' or 'an' can only be singular.
- The indefinite article 'a' is usually used in front of words beginning with a consonant (that is, a letter of the alphabet that is not one of the five vowels: a, e, i, o, u).
  a bill a cushion a dog a ferry a gardener a jigsaw
- The indefinite article 'an' is usually used in front of words that start with one of the five vowels (a, e, i, o, u).
  an avalanche an egg an illness an owl an umbrella

- However, when words beginning with 'u' are pronounced with a 'you' sound, then 'a' is used.

  a union a unique experience a uniform a universe

- Words that start with a silent 'h' are treated like words that start with a vowel and therefore require 'an'

  an honour an hour an honest man

✓ *Checkpoint E*

Read the following newspaper report. Choose which version of the indefinite article, 'a' or 'an', is correct where indicated.

AVALANCHE KILLS FIVE

A/An ski resort was devastated yesterday when a/an huge avalanche enveloped it, killing at least five people. A/An fleet of ambulances was immediately sent to the famous town of Fugel in Austria.

'This is a/an unfortunate accident,' said a resort spokesman. 'We were given only a/an hour's warning about a/an unavoidable disaster and there was very little we could do.'

A/An authoritative source estimated damage to the resort would amount to millions of pounds. 'A/An unqualified disaster,' said the Mayor of Fugel.

WHO IS DOING WHAT TO WHOM?

▪ NOUNS AS SUBJECTS

Read the following sentence:

> <u>Customers</u> must not smoke in the store.
> *subject*

- In this sentence, the nouns are 'customers' and 'store'. These nouns are arranged in a certain order within the sentence and perform different **functions**.

- The noun 'customers' is the **subject** of the sentence. It is they who 'must not smoke in the store'. The sentence is about their action, therefore 'customers' is the **subject** of the sentence.

  Here is another sentence:

> The <u>agent</u> recommended the house to the buyers.
> *subject*

The noun 'agent' is the **subject** of the sentence. It is 'the agent' who does the recommending. The sentence is about the action of the agent in recommending the house.

- Sometimes the subject of a sentence is two or more words.

    The <u>government</u> and the <u>motoring organisations</u> agree on this issue.
        subject   *subject*

    In this sentence the nouns 'government' and 'motoring organisations' form the combined **subject** of the sentence.

    <u>Joan</u> and her <u>parents</u> are going on holiday together.
    subject *subject*

    In this sentence the proper noun 'Joan' and the common noun 'parents' form the combined **subject**.

    <u>Flour</u>, <u>eggs</u>, <u>salt</u> and <u>water</u> are essential ingredients.

    In this sentence the combined subject consists of four nouns: 'flour, eggs, salt and water'.

    Here is another sentence:

    <u>Fairness</u> is essential with kids.
     subject

    The abstract noun 'fairness' is the subject of the sentence.

- The *word order* of this sentence could be rearranged in this way:

    With kids, <u>fairness</u> is essential.

    If we put 'With kids' at the beginning of the sentence, we are perhaps slightly changing the emphasis of the sentence. The subject of a sentence need not appear at the beginning of a sentence. For example, here are some sentences in which the subject is not present in the first words.

    However, the <u>opposite</u> could be true.
            subject

    Slowly and gradually, the <u>tortoise</u> reached his goal.
                subject

    In the event of my death, all my <u>wealth</u> becomes yours.
                    subject

✓ *Checkpoint F*

1 Make a list of or circle the nouns that are used as subjects in the following advertisement.

So you're tired of breakfast cereals!

Shoppers in supermarkets are faced with an amazing choice of breakfast cereals. Flakes and mueslis crowd the shelves. Inevitably, a certain sameness creeps in.

But now a genuinely new product is on the market.

TIGERCRUNCH is a mixture of muesli, clusters, flakes and bisk all rolled into one delicious treat.

Its ratio of vitamins is second to none. Fibre leaps from its every grain. Healthy eating **AND** enjoyment can now return to your breakfast table.

So don't delay. Get **TIGERCRUNCH** today. Breakfasts will never be 'samey' again.

2 Read the following magazine article. Make a list of or circle only the nouns that are used as the subjects of sentences.

Autographs of the famous are big business nowadays. The signature of a dead movie star such as Marilyn Monroe or Humphrey Bogart can fetch thousands of pounds at auction. Famous statesmen such as Winston Churchill also attract rich collectors of autographs. Indeed, if you want to get into the big league of autograph-hunting, then money talks.

Inevitably, the point of this craze is queried. The secret is simple. Collectors buy a piece of the famous person with his or her autograph. Of course, auction-houses and dealers fan the craze. Big bucks are involved in the business. Investors and speculators are even buying up autographs as red-hot investments. Dead film stars seem to be the best bet. If they're dead, the stars cannot sign any more autographs! Scarcity boosts prices!

Activity 3

Write a mini-story of no more than 100 words with the title 'The Celebrity'. Every sentence has to use a noun as its subject.

▪ NOUNS AS OBJECTS

- Nouns are very often the subject of a sentence. The subject of a sentence is the person, thing, quality, idea or action that the sentence is about.
- Nouns can also be the **object** of a sentence. The object of a sentence is the person, thing, quality, idea or action that is acted upon.
- Whereas every complete sentence has a subject, not all sentences have an object. Here are some sentences with objects:

    <u>She'll</u> be bathing the <u>baby</u>.
    subject   *object*

The action of 'bathing' is done to the 'baby', so 'baby' is the **object** of the action and of the sentence.

    <u>Lorry-drivers</u> love <u>chocolate</u>.
    subject   *object*

What the lorry-drivers love, 'chocolate', is the **object** of the sentence.

Undoubtedly the <u>children</u> possessed an acute <u>intelligence</u>.
        subject   *object*

The act of possessing is done to 'the **intelligence**', so that abstract noun is the **object** of the sentence.

- Just as there can be two or more subjects to a sentence, so there can be **two or more objects**.

The host greeted <u>Margaret and Joe</u> with great warmth.
                combined object

The supermarket was selling <u>bread</u>, frozen <u>fish</u> and <u>shampoo</u> at very low prices.

In this sentence, 'bread', 'fish' and 'shampoo' form the **combined object**.

✓ *Checkpoint G*

Read the following notice and make a list of or circle the nouns that are used as objects.

Visiting the Czech Republic

PASSPORTS: British passport holders do not require visas. They must, however, possess a passport valid for at least six months after their planned date of return home.

LANGUAGE: Many Czech people speak German and English.

CURRENCY: Visitors must bring travellers cheques or sterling to exchange for koruna.

CREDIT CARDS: Most hotels and restaurants accept Visa, Access, Amex and Diners Club.

LOCAL GOODS: We recommend crystal, porcelain and liqueurs.

POSTAGE: Postcards must have stamps worth five koruna; letters require stamps of at least eight koruna.

TRANSPORT: Buses and trams have an efficient network and regular service.

Activities 4 and 5

4 Fill in the gaps in the following sentences with an appropriate noun which will be the object of the sentence.
   a) The anxious mother telephoned her .... late one night.
   b) The police were seeking .... about a particular suspect.
   c) Jubilantly, the supporters celebrated the .... of their team.
   d) Nevertheless, the government will introduce .... and .... by the autumn.
   e) The train left the .... promptly.

5 Write a mini-story of no more than 100 words with the title 'The Imposter'. In each sentence use at least one noun as the object of the sentence.

▪ **NOUNS AS INDIRECT OBJECTS**

- We have looked at the use of nouns as the subjects and objects of sentences.
- Nouns can also perform the function of **indirect object** in sentences.
- What is an indirect object? The object of a sentence, remember, is the person, thing or feeling that an action is done to. The indirect object is the person, thing or feeling **for whom** or **to whom** an action is done.

> *YOUNG POLICEMAN TELLS PARENTS THE TRAGIC NEWS*

- 'Policeman' is the **subject** of this sentence (he does the telling).
- 'News' is the **object** (it has the telling done to it).
- 'Parents' is the **indirect object** (the action of the telling of the news is done to them).
- To see more clearly which is the indirect object, turn the sentence around : Young policeman tells the tragic news <u>to parents</u>.

> **The restaurant will serve customers afternoon tea between 2 p.m. and 4.30 p.m.**

In this sentence, 'restaurant' is the **subject** (it will do the serving), 'afternoon tea' is the **object** (it has the serving done to it), and 'customers' is the **indirect object** (it is for them the serving is done).

> The agency will sell
> individual applicants
> tickets for
> # Mad live
> from
> the 21st of September.

In this sentence, 'agency' is the **subject** (the agency does the selling), 'tickets' is the **object** (the selling is done to the tickets) and 'applicants' is the **indirect object** (they are the people to whom the selling of the tickets is done).

- A sentence can have an indirect object and not have an object.
    He told <u>them</u>.   Write to <u>me</u>.

✓ *Checkpoint H*

Read the following report. There are six examples of nouns as indirect objects. Make a list of these, restricting your choice to six only.

Football authorities are determined to give supporters a fair deal over Cup Final tickets. In the past, ticket touts have made thousands from exploiting scarcity. The football clubs have communicated to the Football Association the information it had demanded. From now on, the clubs must show the authorities all the details about where their allocation of tickets goes. The clubs have sent all their players a reminder about not selling tickets to ticket spivs. Hopefully, these new controls will give genuine followers of the game a better chance of getting tickets for this showpiece of the football season.

SKILLCHECK Check these statements to assess what you have learned from this section. If you cannot honestly tick all of these statements, go back over the relevant section.

❏ I understand what a noun is.

❏ I can recognise abstract, collective and proper nouns.

❏ I understand what the subject of a sentence is.

❏ I understand what the object of a sentence is.

❏ I understand what the indirect object of a sentence is.

2
PRONOUNS
AVOIDING REPETITION

- In this section we are looking at words that can take the place of nouns: pronouns.
- Pronouns help us to avoid repeating ourselves all the time. If we have already referred to a noun by name (e.g. a person or an object), we do not really want to go on repeating the noun:

    I really like Elvis. Elvis is the greatest. Elvis makes great music. Of all singers, I admire Elvis the most.

- Repeating the name of the person like this is unnecessary and tedious, so we can use pronouns instead of the proper name after it has been used once:

    I really like Elvis. <u>He</u> is the greatest. <u>He</u> makes great music. Of all singers, I admire <u>him</u> the most.

- 'I', 'he' and 'him' are all **pronouns**. 'He' and 'him' are taking the place of the proper noun 'Elvis'.

    Here is another sentence where the noun that is the name of an object is unnecessarily repeated:

    The car has a 1600cc engine. The car has a top speed of 110 miles an hour. The car has a fuel consumption that is very economical.

By using pronouns, however, the sentences become much less repetitive:

    The car has a 1600cc engine. It has a top speed of 110 miles an hour. It has a fuel consumption that is very economical.

'It' is a pronoun standing in for the noun 'car'.

✓ *Checkpoint A*

Read the following letter. Make a list of all the sixteen pronouns that are used.

Dear Joe,

The parents are driving me crazy. They are not my idea of fun companions on holiday. We go to bed at around 9.30 just when the discos are getting warmed up. Incidentally, they look great on the island, but, of course, I won't get a chance to get near them. Why are old people so dull? Do you know the answer? I'm never going to be like them. When I reach forty, I will still be raving and you can come with me to discos every night!

How are things with you? I suppose summer in Baykop is not everyone's cup of tea. Still, being with my folks on this Greek island sometimes doesn't feel any different from Baykop!

See you soon.

Iris

TYPES OF PRONOUNS

■ PERSONAL PRONOUNS

The type of pronoun we use most often is the **personal pronoun**.

- **Personal pronouns** take the place of the names of other people (you, he, she, they), ourselves (I, we), animals (he, she, they, it), and things (it, they):

I'm with the Ipswich

IT CAME FROM

OUTER

SPACE

They said this film would never be made...

We are the greatest!

You'll never walk alone...

| I | we | you | she | he | it | they |

These are all personal pronouns.
- All the personal pronouns used in the examples above are the **subjects** of the sentence.
- When personal pronouns are used as the **objects** or **indirect objects** of sentences, then most of them take a different form.

I becomes **me**   **we** becomes **us**   **he** becomes **him**
she becomes **her**   **they** becomes **them**

- Only **you** and **it** remain the same in the object form.
  Here are some examples of personal pronouns used as objects or indirect objects in sentences:

To know me is to love me ♥♥♥

Vote for Sleaze Trust him!

The world doesn't owe us a living.

We made them with **You** *in mind!*

Activity 1

Read the following dialogue. Gaps have been left which should be filled in with an appropriate personal pronoun.

JIM .... am bored. Bored, bored, bored!
JANET .... are bored? .... bet .... am more bored. Switch on the telly.
JIM Switch .... on yourself. Anyway ....'s boring. Let's phone Sue and Bill.
JANET Why? .... never phone .... bore .... and .... bore .... phone .... if .... like.
JIM A film would cheer .... up.
JANET .... went to the cinema last night. .... ought to see my mother. .... owe .... a phone call.
JIM Talk about boring!
JANET What about your father? In the boredom stakes, there's no beating ....
JIM There .... go again! Always complaining.
JANET Boredom! Complaining helps relieve ....

■ MORE ABOUT PERSONAL PRONOUNS

Personal pronouns after prepositions

- **Prepositions** are those little words that are usually placed before a phrase to show the position of something or the direction of a movement:
  in a garden   at a party,   behind a wall,
  towards victory   from the house
  You will find much more about prepositions in Section 6.

- When a personal pronoun follows a preposition, the **object form** of the personal pronoun is used:

me   us   you   him   her   it   them

Here are some examples:
  They're talking about us.
  Buy one from me!
  They said she was evil, they were all against her, except for one man . . .
  Gossips! Never listen to them!

I and me

- A common mistake is to confuse 'I' and 'me':
  Our friends met Jack and I as usual.
  Jack and me went to the theatre.
  'Jack and I' form the combined **object** of the first sentence, so the object form '**me**' should be used.
  In the second sentence, 'Jack' and 'me' is the combined **subject** of 'went' so the **subject** form of the pronoun '**I**' should be used.

- To help you to choose which form to use, try leaving out the other person. 'Our friends met I' clearly sounds wrong, as does 'me went to the cinema'.

- The correct form alone is the same correct form in combination.

- Another common error is to place 'I' and 'me' in front of other people:
  They blamed me and my brother.
  I and my sister went to the concert.

- The other person should always come before 'I' or 'me'.
  They blamed my brother and me.
  My sister and I went to the concert.

Activity 2

Read the following extract from a personal diary. There are several errors in it. Rewrite the extract using the pronouns in the correct form.

> **JUNE 21**
>
> Jackie came over in the afternoon and she went with Tony and I to the club. Me and Jackie enjoyed ourselves but Tony was down. He asked Jackie and I to go to a dance on Thursday. Jackie and me said no. While me and Jackie were having a chat, this bloke sat behind me and her. He said he liked the look of I, but I told him to get lost. Came home and made me and Jackie some tea. Then me and Jackie watched some telly. Went to bed early.

■ POSSESSIVE PRONOUNS

- **Possessive pronouns** are used in the place of nouns to indicate ownership.
- The **possessive pronouns** are:

mine   ours   yours   hers   his   its   theirs

- **Possessive pronouns** should not be confused with **possessive adjectives**, words such as my, our, your, her, his, their.
- Possessive adjectives are placed in front of a noun.
- Possessive pronouns take the place of a noun:

because you're mine...

MP ADMITS SHARES WERE HIS!

Ours is the Right

HIS 'n' HERS

I'll see to *theirs*, you see to *yours* and she'll see to *hers*.

In each of the above sentences, the possessive pronouns take the place of • noun.

• Using possessive pronouns avoids unnecessary repetition.

Activities 3 and 4

3 Read the following dialogue. Gaps have been left which you should fill with the appropriate possessive pronoun.

| mine   ours   yours   his   hers   its   theirs |

HEAD   We have our standards at this school. No doubt you have .... at home as well.

PARENT Standards! You worry about .... , leave .... alone.

HEAD   Yes, but your son has to meet .... Not the standards of a street gang. The standard of behaviour we want from him is .... , not ....

PARENT The right to teach my son standards is .... , not ....

HEAD   I have to disagree. It is .... , not .... alone nor .... alone.

PARENT A school has its standards, a family does too.

HEAD   Perhaps we could hope for agreement on standards between the two. Our standards can be yours, and ....

PARENT We'll shake on that.

4 The following report of a football match is unnecessarily repetitive. There are occasions where the use of possessive pronouns would improve the writing. Rewrite the report using possessive pronouns where you think it is appropriate.

DAWLEY PLUNGE — TO DEFEAT —

Crisis once again hit Dawley Town as they plunged to their 25th successive defeat at Brighton today. 'The responsibility for this state of affairs is my responsibility,' said 'Hacker' Brown, the team coach. 'The choice of players is my choice. I have my opinions, the board have their opinions. The players also have their opinions. The supporters have their moans about me, I have my moans about them.'

The latest 6–0 defeat has left the club well adrift at the bottom of the league. 'The manager should listen to ideas from the supporters,' said one lifelong Dawley supporter. 'The trouble is he has his ideas, the supporters have their ideas. The supporters have their priorities, the club has its priorities.'

▪ RELATIVE PRONOUNS

The **relative pronouns** are:

| who whom whose which that |

- A **relative pronoun** relates one part of a sentence to another and also stands in for a noun or another pronoun.
Consider these two sentences:

In the first notice, there are two parts to the sentence: the different parts are joined by 'and' and the pronoun 'it' stands in for the noun 'estate'. In the second, the two parts are joined by the **relative pronoun** 'which'; it joins the two parts of the sentence together, taking the place of 'and it'.

> *Carrot Homes announces the construction of a new estate and it will be very spacious and of high quality.*

> *Carrot Homes announces the construction of a new estate, which will be very spacious and of high quality.*

Here is another example:
  She is a superstar and I admire her very much.
  She is a superstar whom I admire very much.

In the first sentence, 'and' joins the two parts of the sentence together. The pronoun 'her' refers to 'superstar'.
In the second one the **relative pronoun** 'whom' takes the place of 'and' as a joining word and stands in for the pronoun 'her'.

- Note that it is 'whom' rather than 'who' because 'her' is the **object** of the verb 'admire' and therefore the **object form** 'whom' has to be used.
- **who** and **whom** refer to **people**, **which** refers to **things**. **Whose** indicates **possession**:
  These are the people <u>whose</u> house was burnt down.
  They belonged to a club <u>whose</u> members were fanatical about fitness.
- **That**, when it is a relative pronoun, can be used for either **things** or **people**:
  He is the man <u>that</u> broke the bank at Monte Carlo.
  This building is one <u>that</u> has a preservation order on it.
- **Whom**, the object form of **who**, is the form that is used **after prepositions** (see Personal pronouns after prepositions on page 28):
  Do not ask <u>for whom</u> the bell tolls, it tolls for thee.
  <u>To whom</u> are you addressing that remark, sir?
  Officer, the lady <u>with whom</u> I was travelling has disappeared.
  He was definitely the kind of guy <u>about whom</u> people talk.
The above sentences are the grammatically correct versions. In spoken

English it is now quite usual, however, to use **who** and put the **preposition** at the end of a clause (the part of the sentence):

Do not ask <u>who</u> the bell tolls <u>for</u>, it tolls for thee.
<u>Who</u> are you addressing that remark <u>to</u>, sir?
Officer, the lady <u>who</u> I was travelling <u>with</u> has disappeared.
He was definitely the kind of guy <u>who</u> people talk <u>about</u>.

Indeed, in the last two examples above, the relative pronouns would probably be dropped:

Officer, the lady I was travelling with has disappeared.
He was definitely the kind of guy people talk about.

Activities 5 and 6

5 Read the following short article about video games. It is made up of sentences consisting of two parts joined either by 'and' or 'but'. Each of the sentences could be shortened by the use of a relative pronoun. Rewrite the article using a relative pronoun to replace the words that have been underlined.

who	whom	whose	which	that

— ARE OUR KIDS VIDEO-MAD? —

For a number of years now young people have been mesmerised by video games, <u>but now these games</u> are threatening to ruin the lives of youngsters across the nation.

So says a group of worried parents and psychologists <u>and their</u> concern is the amount of time and money teenagers spend on these games. 'Millions are being made from this craze by big companies <u>and they</u> just don't care about young people's health or education,' said one extremely worried parent. Parents are backed up by a group of psychologists <u>and they</u> are calling for government restrictions on advertising video games. 'It's as big a menace as smoking <u>and smoking</u> results in ill-health later in life.' So said one expert, <u>but he</u> refused to be named. Justin Dollars, a spokesman for Mindless Pastimes, a leading manufacturer of video games, refuted that statement <u>and</u> he refused to consider <u>it</u> seriously.

6 Fill in the gaps in the following sentences with the correct relative pronoun.
   a) It was a problem about .... they were all worried.
   b) There was only one course of action .... would bring success.
   c) There was still some doubt about .... coat it was.
   d) I liked the house, the kitchen of .... was very well-equipped.
   e) The doctor examined the patient, ... he had seen before.
   f) She contracted an illness for .... there was no remedy.

DEMONSTRATIVE PRONOUNS

- The demonstrative pronouns are:

this	that	these	those

- Demonstrative pronouns take the place of nouns and focus our attention on a particular thing, place, idea or person.
  This is your life!
  Those were the days.
  These are the Wembley heroes!
- The demonstrative pronouns can also be used to make a contrast:
  This is the one we want! (meaning that we don't want any other)
- Often, 'this' and 'these' are used to refer to something closer to us, physically or in time, while 'that' and 'those' are used to refer to something more distant.
  That was then, this is now.
  This is the right turning, we don't want that one.
- When 'this' or 'that', 'these' or 'those' are placed in front of a noun, as in 'that one' in the last example, they are **demonstrative adjectives**. (There is more about this in Section 4).
  This knife is mine, that one is yours.
  These potatoes should go into that pan.
  That joke was the best one you've made yet.
- Again, they can be used to contrast one thing/person/place/idea with another, as in the first example above, or they can be used simply to draw our attention to the item.

A MIXED BAG OF PRONOUNS

- Here is a selection of pronouns that are very commonly used in English:

any	anyone	anybody	anything
each	either	neither	
everybody	everyone	everything	
few	several		
much	more	most	many
no one	none	nobody	nothing
some	someone	somebody	something

- The words that are underlined can be adjectives as well, depending how they are used in a sentence.
  Any will do. (pronoun)
  Any old iron! Any iron at all! (adjective)
  Each has its own style. (pronoun)
  Each competitor has his own style. (adjective)

The following **pronouns** take a **singular verb** when they function as the **subject** of a sentence:

anyone   anybody   anything   everybody   each   either   neither
much   everyone   everything   no one   nobody   nothing
someone   somebody   something

Everyone opts for that.
Either is correct.
Nothing is impossible.
Something is wrong.

Activity 7

Read the following advertisement for an after-dinner chocolate. Gaps have been left in the text which you should fill with an appropriate pronoun from the group listed above.

That Special Dinner Guest

.... *has been invited to dinner.* .... *very
important. You have planned the menu to the last detail.*
.... *is in hand.*

Or is it? .... *is missing. Of course! The after-dinner
chocolates!*

There are .... *in the house. Well, there are, but
they're only cheap mints. Your important guest deserves
better.* .... *else deserves better too. You! After all,*
.... *depends on the impression you make.*

You think, I cancel or slit my throat. .... *is necessary.
Because you know the solution.* **Ferrari Chocco**.
.... *loves* **Ferrari Chocco***. Well,* .... *with taste,
style, discrimination and class. Give yourself and that
special* .... *a treat.* .... *but good will come of it.*

Give your guests **Ferrari Chocco**. .... *will admire
your style. Promise!*

■ INTERROGATIVE PRONOUNS

- The pronouns **who, whom, whose,** and **which** can be used not only as relative pronouns as we have seen on page 31, but also as **interrogative pronouns**, as can **what**.

- They stand in for nouns in sentences that ask questions:

    <u>Which</u> do you want?
    <u>What</u> is the answer?
    <u>Who</u> wrote this book
    <u>Whom</u> do we have to thank for that?
    <u>Whose</u> is this?

- **Which, what** and **whose** can also be used as **adjectives** when they are attached to nouns.

    <u>Which</u> cereal do you want?
    <u>What</u> sort of answer is that?
    <u>Whose</u> fault is that?

✓ *Checkpoint B*

Read the following news report and list the four interrogative pronouns used, giving the next word also.

A Path to
PEACE?

WHAT is the best way to bring about peace in this war-torn country? Which solution has the best chance? That is the problem for the negotiators.

WHO knows the right answer? To whom can the participants in the war turn? Whose responsibility is it ultimately?

THERE are no easy roads to peace. Which is the best road to take? It will need immense goodwill and faith. Which side has the courage to take the first step?

▪ REFLEXIVE PRONOUNS

• The **reflexive pronouns** are:

myself	ourselves	yourself	yourselves	herself	himself	itself
			themselves			

• These pronouns are called reflexive because they **reflect** or refer back to the **subject** of the sentence.

He drove <u>himself</u> crazy with fear!
Heroine Rescues <u>Herself</u>!
Treat <u>yourselves</u> to an awayday!
Derby Winner Proves <u>Itself</u> Again!
Bonnie and Clyde lived for <u>themselves</u> and died by <u>themselves</u>!

In each of these sentences, the underlined pronouns reflect back to the subject of the sentence.

• Sometimes reflexive pronouns are used for emphasis:

I <u>myself</u> have seen the evidence.
We will do the job <u>ourselves</u>.
The solution lies with <u>themselves</u>.

• You must use the appropriate reflexive pronoun to reflect the subject of a sentence:

I	myself	he	himself
we	ourselves	she	herself
you	yourself or yourselves	it	itself
		they	themselves

Activity 8

Read the following note and fill in the gaps with an appropriate reflexive pronoun.

Jill,

Make _____ some supper. I have already eaten.
We must treat _____ to a meal at the weekend.
Eat well and diets take care of _____! The cat
has fed _____ again: a bird from the garden.
Don't upset _____ about it. I'll drive _____ to the
leisure centre.
See you later. Ray

SKILLCHECK Check these statements to assess what you have learned from this section. If you cannot honestly tick every statement, go back over the section.

❏ I understand what function pronouns perform.

❏ I realise that pronouns can be useful in making my speech and writing clearer and less repetitive.

❏ I can tell the difference between pronouns and adjectives.

❏ I am familiar with the various types of pronouns.

❏ I feel confident about using pronouns in my writing.

3
V E R B S
NOT JUST 'DOING' WORDS

- **What are verbs?** A sentence needs a verb:
    Just <u>do</u> it. Everyone <u>screams</u> for ice-cream!
    The car in front <u>is</u> a Coyote.
- The underlined words are the verbs of the sentence. Verbs give a sentence its action, or describe the feeling the person (the subject of the sentence) has.
- Verbs may also be about 'existing' or 'being':

Our competitors may appear attractive, but it is we who are at the cutting edge.

- **Am** is part of the verb **to be**, which is a very important verb in English, since various forms of it are required to indicate the **tense** of a verb (see page 39).

- **Appear** and **seem** do not really express actions, but are still verbs.

- To say that verbs are 'doing words' is a useful idea, but some verbs cannot really be included in that description.

THE VERB 'TO BE'

- The verb 'to be' is a verb in its own right and its different forms are frequently used in speech and writing. It changes its form much more often than most verbs, according to the **person** and the **tense**.

- Present and past tenses of the verb 'to be':

	present tense	*past tense*
First person singular	I am	I was
First person plural	we are	we were
Second person singular/plural	you are	you were
Third person singular	he/she/it is	he/she/it was
Third person plural	they are	they were

- In addition to being a verb in its own right, however, the verb 'to be' is used in its various forms as a **'helping'** or **auxiliary** verb to indicate tense in other verbs:

  I <u>am</u> eating my breakfast at the moment. (continuous present tense)
  She <u>was</u> reading the newspaper when I entered the room. (continuous past tense)
  They <u>were</u> climbing the hill when I met them. (continuous past tense)

  The continuous present or past tenses describe an action that is or was continuing and is not or was not yet complete.

'TO DO' AND 'TO HAVE' – MORE HELPING VERBS

- 'To do' and 'to have' are, like the verb 'to be', verbs in their own right, but they also perform an important role in forming **tenses** of other verbs, or in forming **questions**. They act as helping or **auxiliary** verbs:

a)

HOW
DO
THEY
KNOW
THAT?

b)

Have you
Macbrushed
your teeth
today?

c) **England Have Done It!**

d)

What did you do in the war, Daddy?

In (a) **do** helps to form the question.
In (b) **have** also helps to form a question.
In (c) **have** helps to form the perfect tense of the verb 'to do'.
In (d) **did**, the past tense of 'to do', is used to form a question.

- The verb 'to do' may also be used to emphasise an action:
    I <u>do</u> like to be beside the sea . . .   He <u>does</u> go on and on . . .

- So, we can see that very frequently verbs consist of **more than one word** because there has to be a way of indicating when an action took place, a feeling was experienced or a state of existing occurred.

- Other **auxiliary** verbs are:
    may   might   will   shall   would   should   must
    can   could   need

These can be used with a verb, or with a form of the verbs 'to be' and 'to have' plus another verb, as in these newspaper headlines:

Directors Need Not Pay Creditors Judge Rules

WILL THE REAL TRUTH EVER COME OUT?

HE WOULD SAY THAT, WOULDN'T HE!

We Have Been Duped Claim Holiday Couple

Shadow Chancellor Claims Budget May Increase Taxes

'Scotland CAN Win' Claims Captain

We May Have Blown It, Admits Government Minister

I Shall Appear Despite Ill Health, Claims Star

United Might Lose Says Manager

We Should Have Been Warned, Say Pensioners

Report Shows Travellers Should Have Been Insured

I DARE SAY SAYS SUPERSTAR

✓ *Checkpoint A*

Read the beginning to this short story and pick out the verbs that are used. Some will consist of one word, others will consist of two, three or four words because auxiliary verbs have been used.

The Werewolf

It was midnight on a dark, dark night. Samuel had taken the short cut through the forest. The path was familiar and he felt good as he gazed up at the clear skies with their adornment of bright moon and stars.

Suddenly, there loomed a dark presence in front of him.

'Who is that?' he cried. 'What are you doing? Do I know you, sir?'

The figure raised his head to the moon and howled, an eerie, inhuman, wolflike howl.

Samuel leapt back in fear. Were his eyes and ears deceiving him? Could this creature be human? It looked human and yet, as he saw its features more clearly, he realised the creature's face was covered in a thick fur, which could not be a heavy morning growth of beard.

Samuel knew he should be taking to his heels, but something was holding him there. He was sensing that he had been given the opportunity of encountering the unknown. And the unknown had been a source of fascination to him all his life. This creature might reveal a secret of the unknown world to him.

'Where do you come from? Do you have a purpose?' he asked.

The creature howled again and reached out with a large, hairy paw.

Activity 1

Read the following advertisement for a headache tablet. Gaps have been left in the text which you should fill with appropriate auxiliary verbs. It is indicated how many auxiliary verbs are needed for each gap.

HEADACHE RELIEF

.... you got that important interview coming up? For a job? A complete change of direction? It .... be an important exam.

It .... be challenging anyway. You .... to be at your best. Perhaps you .... have something handy to make sure you do yourself justice. Because headaches .... strike at any time especially when you .... be under pressure.

That's why we .... created **NEUROFREE**. Keep one or two **NEUROFREES** handy and you .... have no more worries. Then the rest .... be up to you.

You .... take a chance. But then, that .... be disastrous for your future. **NEUROFREE**, the pain-killer that .... put you in the driving seat.

MAKING VERBS AGREE

We have already worked on nouns and pronouns as subjects of sentences in Sections 1 and 2.

I TEND TO AGREE WITH HIM!

SUBJECT

VERB

- Verbs have to **agree** with the **subject** of the sentence or the part of the sentence. The form of verbs varies according to who or what is carrying out the action, expressing the feeling or 'being'.

- Two main factors affect the form of the verb: the **person** (first, second or third person) and whether it is **singular** or **plural**.

- For example, consider the verb 'climb'.
  First person present tense:
    I climb   we climb
  Second person present:
    you climb
  Third person present:
    he climb**s**   they climb

- The only difference is in the third person singular when, in common with many other verbs, '**s**' is added to 'climb'.

- In the past tense of 'climb', all persons, singular and plural, end in '**ed**':
  climbed.
  However, with the perfect tense and the continuous past tense, you have to choose between 'has/'have and was' (singular)/were' (plural):
    I <u>have been climbing</u> the mountain. (the action is now **completed**)
    They <u>were climbing</u> the mountain. (this describes a **continuing action in the past**)
    She <u>has climbed</u> the mountain.
    It <u>has climbed</u> through the window.
    I <u>was climbing</u> the Matterhorn.

- Many verbs follow this pattern, but there are also numerous irregular verbs that take different forms. However, the really important point is to remember to make the **subject** and **verb** agree, taking into account person and whether the subject is singular or plural.

- Frequently, there are **combined subjects** of two or more people or things. These subjects take a **plural** verb:
    My aunt and I <u>are going</u> shopping.
    The rain, the heavy pitch and ball <u>are making</u> it hard to play well.

VERBS

3

- **Pronouns** such as 'each, anyone, either, neither, anybody, every' take a **singular** verb:
  Each of them <u>deserves</u> his fair share.
  Either of the two cars <u>is</u> fine by me.
  Every dog <u>has</u> its day.
- **Collective nouns** (see Section 1), as they mean a single group, usually take a **singular** verb:
  The herd <u>has</u> stampeded.
  The flock of birds <u>was</u> heading south.

Activity 2

Read this letter written to a newspaper. There are nine errors of subject–verb agreement. Pick these out and write down the correct version.

> The Editor,
> Redbridge Chronicle,
> Redbridge.
>
> 10 May 1997
>
> Dear Editor,
>
> My friend and I was having an argument about the Empire in Old Street. Perhaps you or a reader can settle it for us. I were arguing that both the Empire and the Palace in North Street was cinemas before they became bingo halls. My friend insist that the Empire were a theatre not a cinema in the old days.
>
> Every one of my friends like reading your newspaper. We especially likes the articles about old Redbridge. The sports page, the local news, the fashion articles and the crossword puzzle also pleases us. You and your reporters has to keep up the good work!
>
> Yours sincerely,
>
> *Rose Bush*
>
> Rose Bush

THE INFINITIVE – A VERB WITHOUT A SUBJECT

- The infinitive form of a verb names the verb. It is preceded by '**to**': to give, to laugh, to run.
- The infinitive has **no subject**. It refers to the general act of doing something. The infinitive acts as the **equivalent of a noun** and therefore can be the subject and object of a sentence.
  To raise taxes at this time would be unpopular.
- 'To raise' is the **infinitive** of the verb 'raise' and in the above sentence it is used as a noun equivalent (the raising), and acts as the **subject**.
  They desperately want to escape.
- 'To escape' is the **infinitive** and acts as a noun equivalent and as the **object** of the sentence.
- All the examples of infinitives we have given so far have been examples of the present infinitive, but infinitives can be in the **past tense** as well: to have found, to have stolen, to have dealt.
  To have tried one's best and lost is no disgrace.
  In this sentence, the **past infinitive** 'to have tried' acts as the **subject** of the sentence.
  I was expecting to have lost all my money in the crash.
  Here, 'to have lost' is the **past infinitive** and acts as the **object** of the sentence.

✓ Checkpoint B

Read the following dialogue. Pick out the examples of both the present and the past infinitives and list them under separate headings.

MUM	I tried to tell them they were too young.
DAD	Too young to be really in love?
MUM	To have done anything else would have been irresponsible. What else was I supposed to do?
DAD	To have done anything else would have been daft.
MUM	Mind you, we wanted to marry at their age.
DAD	And we did. We didn't want to wait.
MUM	To marry in haste is to repent at leisure.
DAD	To have waited years to marry would not have been much fun.
MUM	They have to learn a hard lesson.
DAD	To err is human . . .
MUM	. . . to forgive divine.
DAD	You said it, my dear.

TO DO OR TO BE DONE –
THE ACTIVE AND PASSIVE VOICE

Read the following sentences.

a)
STAR STRIKER SCORES WINNING GOAL.

b)
Winning Goal Was Scored By Star Striker.

- Both of these sentences say more or less the same thing, but there is a different **emphasis** from the manner in which they are written.

- In the first sentence the **subject** is the 'star striker' so the emphasis is on the fact that **he** scored the winning goal.

- In the second one the **subject** is the 'winning goal' so the emphasis is on the **goal** rather than the scorer.
  In the first sentence the subject carries out the action; in the second one, the subject is the recipient of the action, the action is done to it.

- In the first example, then, the verb is in the **active** voice; in the second the verb is in the **passive** voice.
  Here are some more examples to illustrate the difference between the active and passive voices:
  At the Palladium last night, the comedian topping the bill told some very unfunny jokes. (active voice)
  At the Palladium last night, some very unfunny jokes were told by the comedian topping the bill. (passive voice)
  The decorator painted the living room in white vinyl. (active)
  The living room was painted in white vinyl by the decorator. (passive)

Again, in these examples, the pairs of sentences have more or less the same meaning, except that the use of the active or passive voices creates a slightly different emphasis.

Generally, in your own writing you will use the active voice. The active voice is more personal and less formal. There may, however, be occasions when the passive voice is appropriate: when you are writing a report of a scientific experiment, for example, or a formal report. The passive voice can also be used if you want to emphasise a point:

The work <u>was done by me</u>, (not by you).

✓ Checkpoint C

Read the following report of a public opinion survey. List all the verbs used under the headings *Active voice*, *Passive voice* and *Infinitive form*.

BRITAIN PREFERS CATS!

A recent public opinion poll has revealed that the British prefer cats to dogs as domestic pets. Up to now, it was considered that the British were among the leading dog-loving nations of the world, but a poll carried out by Useless Information Pollsters, which was commissioned by the Moggies Defence League, has indicated that 66 per cent of Britons who express a preference prefer cats to dogs.

The poll was conducted amongst 500 residents of Milton Keynes. 60 per cent of households with pets have cats as domestic pets, while it was discovered that only 35 per cent kept dogs. Poodles were named as their least favourite pet by 30 per cent of those interviewed, while hamsters were disliked by three per cent and budgies by two per cent.

'To be frank, the findings of the poll do not surprise us,' said a spokesperson at the Moggies Defence League. 'Cats do not bite postmen, there are no pit bull Persians and moggies do not make a mess in the street.'

Activity 3

Each of the following sentences has a verb in the active voice. Rewrite them changing the verb into the passive voice.
a) The workers earned every penny of their wages.
b) The scientist conducted the experiment under strictly controlled conditions.
c) The gardener cut the lawn with the new mower.
d) The judge found the defendant guilty as charged.
e) The secretary phoned the customer with an apology.

THE TIME OF THE ACTION

- There are three main tenses for verbs to use. The **tense** of the verb in a sentence shows the **time** of the action: **past**, **present** or **future**:

a) It rains every Sunday.
b) It is raining now.

c) It was raining when I arrived.
d) It rained all the time.
e) It has rained every day.
f) It had rained every day but one.

g) It will rain tomorrow.
h) It is going to rain tomorrow.

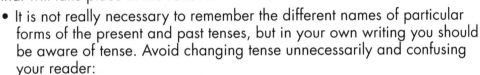

I'M SO TENSE, I DON'T KNOW WHETHER I'M LIVING IN THE PAST, THE PRESENT OR THE FUTURE.

(a) and (b) are examples of sentences describing events in the **present**; (c), (d), (e) and (f) describe events in the **past**; (g) and (h) describe an event that will take place in the **future**.

- It is not really necessary to remember the different names of particular forms of the present and past tenses, but in your own writing you should be aware of tense. Avoid changing tense unnecessarily and confusing your reader:

  I <u>walk</u> down the road and my friend <u>yelled</u> at me from across the street.
  I <u>turn</u> and he <u>crossed</u> the road.

This starts off in the present tense, 'walk', and then, for no apparent reason, changes into the past tense, 'yelled'. Then it changes back into the present, 'turn', and then into the past again, 'crossed'. This is incorrect usage. Make up your mind what tense you want to use and keep to it, except for necessary changes, for example, when you are using verbs in **direct speech**:

  The cowboy <u>rode</u> into town. It <u>was</u> hot and dusty and he <u>needed</u> a drink. He <u>tied</u> his horse outside the town's one saloon and <u>strode</u> through the swing doors.
    'What <u>will</u> you <u>have</u>?' the bartender <u>asked</u>.
    'I <u>am drinking</u> whisky,' <u>said</u> a voice before the newcomer <u>could</u> reply.
    The cowboy <u>turned</u>. He recognised the old-timer beside him.
    'Why, <u>it's</u> Gabby Sidewinder, you old galoot,' <u>said</u> the cowboy.
In this narrative, the story is told in the **past** tense, but tenses change when direct speech is used. There is an example of **continuous present** tense – 'I am drinking whisky' and **simple present** tense, – 'it's'. The story should, however, continue to be told in the past tense, as that tense has been chosen at the beginning.

Activity 4

The writer of the following narrative has decided to use the present tense for effect. Rewrite the passage using the past tense.

The time is midnight. The city is quiet and all the bad guys are home in bed. Somewhere a lonely trumpet player is playing a sad tune. It is quiet, too quiet.

Suddenly, the sound of a bullet shatters the peace. Car tyres screech in the darkness. A body falls to the pavement. It seems that, after all, not all the bad guys are asleep.

Mickey Chandler, private eye, is instantly awake. He can smell trouble a mile away. He reaches out for his automatic and crosses to the window. He scans the empty streets. Out there, there are bad guys to defeat. He is the man for the task. No criminal is safe when Chandler is in the city.

PARTICIPLES

- The **participle** of a verb is the part of the verb that ends in **-ing** or **-ed**, **-en**, **-d** or **-t**.

    running making laughing seeing (present participles)
    broken carried hidden spoilt paid (past participles)

- The present and past participles are used when the tenses of verbs are formed:

    I <u>am running</u> this organisation
    I <u>was making</u> them laugh.
    I <u>have smashed</u> the glass.
    I <u>had hidden</u> the money.
    The pudding <u>was spoilt</u>.

- However, participles cannot be used on their own. They do not take a subject and so cannot be the main verb in a sentence.

    <u>Knowing</u> the facts as I do, I made the right decision.

    'Knowing' is a **present participle** acting like an adjective because it is describing 'I'.

    <u>Stunned</u> by the news, their mother gathered her courage together.

    Here in this sentence, the **past participle** 'stunned' describes mother.

- Present and past **participles** can also be used exactly like **adjectives** and placed next to the noun they are describing:

    <u>Broken</u> masonry littered the courtyard.
    <u>Amazing</u> scenes were witnessed that night.
    It is a case of <u>burnt</u> offerings, I'm afraid.
    A <u>threatening</u> crowd filled the square.

✓ *Checkpoint D*

Read the following advertisement and list all the present and past participles that are used.

THINKING OF A SUMMER HOLIDAY?

* Bored with Disneyland? Not carried away by the Costa del Astronomical?

* Tired of foreign parts, more and more Britons are holidaying at home. Disappointing ventures into the unknown have led to a reappraisal of what a good holiday means.

* The surprising thing is, Bolton may be just what you're after. Reeling from the shock, you may have thrown this ad away by now. But, no, you're too shrewd for that.

* Considering the options, you may feel Bolton is a good bet. No thwarted dreams. No fleeced pockets. Just simple and honest pleasures. Northern style.

* Bolton, the smart holiday choice. Watching your friends depart for an expensive holiday in the South of France, you'll feel superior. Believe us. Make Bolton your choice this year.

WHEN A THING ENDS IN '-ING'

- Sometimes a word that looks like a present participle of a verb is actually playing the role of a noun.
- A verb used as a noun is called a **gerund**.
- Gerunds end in **-ing**, like the present participle form of the verb (see page 48).

SMOKING IS FORBIDDEN ✖

Dodging fares is liable
to cost you dear

Jo**gg**i**ng** is a craze for crazies

In these sentences 'smoking', 'jogging' and 'dodging' are gerunds, because they are used like nouns.

49

However, consider this sentence:
I was <u>jogging</u> along when I saw
a man <u>smoking</u>.

- In this sentence the '-ing' words are not
  used like nouns. They are a part of
  the verbs in the sentence and they
  have a subject ('I', 'a man'). They are
  participles.

- If you are in any doubt about whether
  a word ending in '-ing' is a participle
  or a gerund, ask yourself how the word
  is used in the sentence. If it is used like a
  noun, then it is a gerund.
  Read the following sentences. One of
  them is grammatically correct, the
  other is incorrect.
  They were amazed by <u>their
  winning</u> the game.
  They were amazed by <u>them winning</u> the game.

- 'Winning' in both sentences is used as a **noun**; it is a gerund. Because
  'winning' is equivalent to a noun, it can only be described by an
  adjective. It requires the **possessive adjective** 'their', not the pronoun
  'them'. So, the first sentence is the correct version.

✓ Checkpoint E

1 Read the following
advertisement and
pick out eight gerunds
(verbs used as nouns)
that have been used in
the text. Restrict your
choice to eight words
only.

CATSNACK
the cat food that cats WON'T refuse

- Tired of putting the same old cat food in front
  of jaded pets?
- Fed up of feeling guilty when your cat turns up
  his or her nose yet again?
- Well, dreading cat mealtimes can be a thing of
  the past. There's a new cat food on the block
  and cats are demanding it already!

**Yes, it's CATSNACK, the revolutionary cat
food that will silence their complaining.**

Choosing CATSNACK will be easy because loving
your cat is easy. Letting them down is not
something you like doing. So junk the competition.
Bringing back happy pet mealtimes is a must.

Choose CATSNACK. Or else . . .

2 Read the following public notice. Several gerunds are used in the text. In front of some of these gerunds there is a choice between two words, a possessive adjective and a pronoun. Choose the grammatically correct word.

AVOIDING PAYMENT OF FARES

It is an offence to travel on the underground system with the intention of avoiding paying. Passengers who pay fares are being penalised by fare-dodgers. Them/Their travelling for nothing means you pay for their/them dodging. You/Your paying out more money for higher fares is not something we want. If you know one of these dodgers, tell them to stop their/them cheating. It's in your interest.

SKILLCHECK   Check these statements to assess what you have learned from this section. If you cannot honestly tick every statement, go back over the section.

❏ I understand what a verb is and what function it performs in a sentence.

❏ I realise that there has to be a subject–verb agreement in sentences.

❏ I know what auxiliary verbs are and the principal ways of using them.

❏ I understand about the present and past infinitives.

❏ I know the difference between the active and passive voices of verbs.

❏ I know what the present and past participles are and how to use them.

❏ I can distinguish gerunds from present participles and know how they are used.

❏ I know that a gerund is equivalent to a noun and so can only be described by an adjective.

4

ADJECTIVES

ADDING INFORMATION TO NOUNS

- **Adjectives are words used to describe a noun.**
- **They give us more information about the thing, place, person or idea named by the noun.**
- **They may also be used to describe pronouns.**
- **Adjectives can either go immediately before their noun, or after the verb and be detached from the noun.**
  They are energetic children.   The children are energetic.
  They are energetic.
- **Appropriately used, adjectives add detail to your writing and make it more lively and interesting.**

Read these two passages.
a) The cottage for let is situated in the heart of the countryside. It is in the village of Graval. The villagers welcome visitors.
b) The pretty and well-furnished cottage for let is situated in the heart of the beautiful French countryside. It is in the tiny village of Graval. The friendly villagers welcome foreign visitors.

The difference between (a) and (b) is that **adjectives** (seven in all) have been added to (b).

- **Adjectives describe nouns** and add information.

- They provide detail and give life to your writing.
  We know more about the cottage and the village in the passage because of these adjectives:
  pretty   well-furnished   beautiful   French   tiny   friendly   foreign

- In your own writing, you should try to find opportunities to use adjectives when it is appropriate to do so.

- Adjectives are attached to nouns and pronouns but they are not always placed in front of nouns.
  The weather was perfect and the playing pitch was green and lush.
  Nevertheless, the match was dreary and unexciting.
  The adjectives used in these sentences are:
  perfect   playing   green   lush   dreary   unexciting
- Only one of them, 'playing', comes in front of the noun it is describing. The rest come after the verb and are detached from the noun they are describing.
- Adjectives can be used singly, in twos, threes or in multiples:

Brave Bystander Has A Go

She was poised, confident and witty.

Latest London Styles Are Hit With Critics

Smooth, handsome, deceiving and ruthless salesman cheats widows.

- It is best not to over-use adjectives by having strings of them attached to a noun or pronoun. On the other hand, where it enhances your writing, you should seek to use adjectives that suit the context, but which are not so familiar that they have no impact. For example, avoid using adjectives such as 'nice, lovely, great, awful' too often.
- Try to expand the range of adjectives you use.

USING NOUNS AS ADJECTIVES

- Adjectives are **describing words** that describe nouns or pronouns. Nouns themselves can, however, function as adjectives depending on their function in a sentence.
  For example, read the following sentences:
  Motor-bike rider was doing ninety!
  Town centre is to be redeveloped
  The computer program nobody could understand!
- The nouns 'motor-bike', 'town' and 'computer' are used in these examples to describe other nouns. They tell us more about the 'rider', 'centre' and 'program'. They are used to describe and therefore, although they are **nouns**, they are **used as adjectives**. You will probably find opportunities in your own writing to use nouns as adjectives.

✓ Checkpoint A

Read the following report and make a list of all the words used as adjectives.

VIOLENT FANS IN PITCH INVASION

A Premier League match between Baykop and Butterworth United was abandoned yesterday because of the intrusion of excited and angry fans onto the pitch at Shamall Lane.

Several policemen struggled with the unruly hooligans to clear the playing area. Astonished players watched the unhappy scene with absolute dismay.

'I was flabbergasted and sick as a parrot,' said the Butterworth, million-pound striker, Albert Entwhistle. 'Out-of-control youngsters like these should be banned.'

A bitter and disenchanted spokesman for the Baykop club said this was the second time visiting fans had invaded the pitch this season. 'It's disgraceful and unacceptable,' the anonymous spokesman stated. 'It's a very serious situation for the club and for the football league as a whole.'

The match replay has been scheduled for next Tuesday.

Activities 1 and 2

1 Read the following opening to a story. Several adjectives are used which are underlined. They are over-familiar and rather unimaginative. Rewrite this opening, replacing the underlined adjectives with other, more suitable words.

The Ghost of the College

The college building was <u>big</u> and <u>dark</u>.

'Cor,' said Julie, 'it's not very <u>nice</u>, is it? I expected something a bit more <u>interesting</u>.'

'I expect it will look better in <u>full</u> daylight,' said Jason.

'What was that?' shouted Julie.

'What?'

An owl hooted. It sounded <u>bad</u> and not <u>nice</u>. A dog barked a <u>loud</u> bark.

'This is not <u>good</u>,' said Julie. 'Let's get away from this <u>bad</u> place.'

2 Now continue 'The Ghost of the College' as you wish, using as many adjectives as you think appropriate to add atmosphere and detail to your short story.

TYPES OF ADJECTIVES

■ QUALITY OR QUANTITY?

- The most common type of adjective is the adjective of **quality**. Adjectives of quality describe some quality or feature that a thing or person possesses:

    blue   clever   round   incredible   lazy

- Then there are adjectives of **quantity**:

    many   a thousand   four   most   more   some   several   little   few

■ DEMONSTRATIVES

- Demonstrative adjectives point out something:

    this   that   these   those

Remember these words are also demonstrative pronouns (see Section 2); they are used as adjectives when they are attached to a noun:

I asked <u>those people</u> over there to move.
<u>That model</u> is the one I want.
<u>These tomatoes</u> are rotten.
<u>This book</u> is very instructive.

■ POSSESSIVES

Possessive adjectives describe **ownership**:

    my   our   your   his   her   its   their

**YOUR
COUNTRY
NEEDS
YOU**

our ice cream is *probably* the best in the world!

|MOTHER RESCUES|
HER CHILDREN

I did it my way! ♪♩

A note about the difference between 'its' and 'it's'

- These two words are commonly confused and used incorrectly. Remember that '**its**' without the apostrophe is the **possessive adjective**:

    The vet was worried because <u>its</u> nose was warm. (its = belonging to it)
    <u>Its</u> crankshaft has gone. (belonging to it)

'It's' is the abbreviated form for '**it is**'; this is the one that has the apostrophe because the 'i' of 'is' has been missed out.

    <u>It's</u> a terrible shame.
    The match has been postponed because <u>it's</u> raining.

- The reason they are so commonly confused is that all the other possessives do have apostrophes – this is the only irregularity. (cat's, grandfather's)

▪ INTERROGATIVES

- **Interrogative adjectives** ask a **question**, but they must be attached to a noun to be classed as adjectives (see Interrogative pronouns on page 35):

    which   what   whose
    <u>Which path</u> is the right one?
    <u>Whose book</u> is this?
    <u>What kind</u> of a man are you?

▪ OTHER ADJECTIVES

- These are all adjectives when they are attached to a noun:

    each   every   either   neither   no   all   any   own

✓ *Checkpoint B*

Read the following letter and make separate lists of adjectives used in it under these headings: *quality, quantity, possessive, demonstrative, interrogative, others.*

Dear Helen,

Back to wonderful old school, eh? The summer holidays already seem a distant prospect.

This year is really important, isn't it? What subjects are you studying? Do you find that every teacher says their subject is the crucial one to pass? Anyway, many nights of homework lie ahead. I have to study four nights a week, plus the lousy weekend. All work and no play make for boredom. It's just not possible to keep it up.

Any chance of you being down my way soon? Our town now boasts a spanking new leisure centre, plus a multiplex cinema. But these days I don't get much chance to get to them,

See you soon, I hope,

Yours sincerely,

Iris

Activity 3

In the following advertisement 'it's and 'it's' have been frequently, but not always, incorrectly used. Rewrite the advertisement, correcting the mistakes.

Its the only shoe to choose

What is style in a shoe?
Its a combination of colour, shape, quality and sheen.

You can tell a really good shoe by the leather on its upper and on it's sole. Its a matter of taste, of course, but then you wouldn't be thinking about buying Bond Shoes if its not good taste you're after.

A Bond shoe has it's own distinctive style, its own subtle sheen, it's own indefinable quality.

For the man who cares about his feet, its always going to be Bond. After all, its a matter of a lifelong **Bond**.

USING ADJECTIVES TO COMPARE

Consider the adjective 'tall':

In this sentence 'tall' is the ordinary form of the adjective.

- In this sentence, 'taller' is used to **compare two** people: one is taller than the other. This form of the adjective 'tall' is called the **comparative**.
- Adjectives that consist of a single syllable usually form the comparative by adding **-er**:
  high higher   small smaller   light lighter   dark darker
- Adjectives are also used to compare **more than two** things. The **superlative** form then has to be used:

- Adjectives that consist of a single syllable usually form their **superlative** by adding **-est**:
  high highest   small smallest   light lightest   dark darkest
- Two-syllable adjectives that end in '-y', '-e' or '-er' also form their comparative and superlative forms by adding '-er' in the comparative and '-est' in the superlative. The '-y' changes to an 'i' as it does in single-syllable adjectives:
  happy   happier   happiest
  lucky   luckier   luckiest
  dry   drier   driest
  able   abler   ablest
  clever   cleverer   cleverest

- Adjectives that consist of one syllable with a consonant at the end and one vowel before this final consonant have to double the final letter before adding '-er' and '-est':
  fit   fitter   fittest
  big   bigger   biggest
  hot   hotter   hottest
- Other two-syllable adjectives and adjectives of more than two syllables form their comparatives by putting 'more' in front, and their superlative by adding 'most':
  reliable (3 *syllables*)   more reliable   most reliable
  worried (2 *syllables*)   more worried   most worried
  comfortable (4 *syllables*)   more comfortable   most comfortable
  interesting (4 *syllables*)   more interesting   most interesting

■ IRREGULAR ADJECTIVES

- There are several adjectives that do not follow any of these rules. These adjectives are **irregular**:
  many/much   more   most
  good   better   best
  little   less   least
  bad   worse   worst
  many   more   most
- There are other irregular adjectives. You probably use some correctly without thinking about them. Try to notice and remember them in your own speech and writing and in those of others.

Activity 4

Read the following dialogue. Replace each adjective in brackets with the correct comparative or superlative.

JAN   This is the (boring) film I've ever seen. Have you ever seen a (bad) movie?
DAVE I have to admit it could be (exciting).
JAN   It was your idea to see it. You could have chosen a (good) film.
DAVE And we could have paid for (cheap) seats.
JAN   I wish I was a bit (slim).
DAVE What? That's the (little) of our worries.
JAN   I want to be (attractive).
DAVE I want to be (rich). The (wealthy) person in the whole world.
JAN   That's the (daft) thing I've ever heard. What about being the (happy) person in the world? That's (much) like it.
DAVE Do you want to see the rest of this movie?
JAN   I'd rather watch paint dry. It would be (interesting).
DAVE This was supposed to be the (funny) film ever made.
JAN   Funny? They must think we're (stupid) than we are.

SKILLCHECK Check these statements to assess what you have learned from this section. If you cannot honestly tick every statement, go back over the section.

❏ I understand what adjectives are.

❏ I can recognise these types of adjectives: adjectives of quality and quantity possessive, demonstrative and interrogative adjectives.

❏ I know what the comparative and superlative forms of adjectives are.

❏ I realise that adjectives form their comparatives and superlatives in various ways.

❏ I know that some adjectives form their comparatives and superlatives in an irregular manner.

5

A D V E R B S

A D D I N G   I N F O R M A T I O N
T O   V E R B S

- **Adverbs give us more information about verbs.**
- **They describe verbs by telling us more about the action of the verb.**
- **They often tell us how the verb took place – this may mean when, in what way, where, how much.**
- **They may also describe adjectives or other adverbs.**
- **Many adverbs end in -ly. Many do not. Some words are sometimes adverbs, at other times they are prepositions or adjectives. To identify an adverb you have to understand its function in the sentence.**

HOW SOMETHING IS DONE

- **Adverbs** are usually attached to verbs and tell us more about them:
    Drive <u>slowly</u> through the village.
  'Slowly' in this sentence is an adverb attached to the verb 'drive'; it tells us 'how' the car should be driven. It is, therefore, an **adverb of manner**.
- Adverbs usually end in **-ly** but not always. Adverbs are usually formed by adding '-ly' to the adjective:
    slow/slowly   great/greatly   immediate/immediately.
- When the adjectives ends in '-y' the adverb is formed by changing 'y' to 'i' and adding '-ly':
    pretty/prettily   lazy/lazily   crazy/crazily.
- Adjectives that end in 'le' form their adverb by dropping their final letter and adding '-ly':
    terrible/terribly   simple/simply   justifiable/justifiably   noble/nobly
    double/doubly
- Many adverbs do not end in '-ly':

about	almost	enough	far	fast	much	more	most	never	not
perhaps	quite	rather	so	sometimes	twice	very	well

| Never take more than the standard dose. | Delivery takes <u>about</u> two weeks. |

They felt <u>quite</u> hungry.

In this last sentence the adverb 'quite' is attached to the adjective 'hungry'. It tells us the degree to which they were hungry.

- So, adverbs, although they are usually attached to verbs, can modify the meaning of adjectives as well, and even of other adverbs:

    He was sentenced <u>incredibly</u> harshly by the judge.

    'Incredibly' modifies the meaning of the adverb 'harshly'.

✓ Checkpoint A

Read the following article and make a list of or circle all the adverbs that are used in it.

SOAP STAR'S TERRIBLE ANGUISH

Jane Evans, who plays Felicity Fanfare in the television soap 'Heritage', talked emotionally and frankly to me yesterday about being suddenly axed from the show.

'Truthfully, it was quite the biggest shock of my life,' she told me, too overcome with emotion to hide her tears successfully. 'I am badly shocked and deeply hurt. I have given myself completely to the show and I am sure my fans will be very upset that the producers have ruthlessly dropped me like this.'

I put it to her directly that the show had been falling alarmingly in the ratings. She looked me straight in the eye in that exceedingly familiar Felicity Fanfare sort of way and argued persuasively that recent scripts had been terribly feeble.

'I have always behaved totally professionally in relation to "Heritage",' she added proudly. 'I am utterly sick that the producers of the show have not been equally professional.'

Activity 1

Fill in each of the gaps in the following sentences with an appropriate adverb of manner:

    a) She struck the ball .... and it flew .... over the net.

    b) The train chugged .... into the station.

    c) The lion roared .... and the keeper reacted ....

    d) The crowd cheered .... when the singer bounded .... onto the stage.

    e) .... , there is absolutely no hope.

OTHER TYPES OF ADVERBS

- So far in this section we have been concentrating on **adverbs of manner**: those adverbs that tell us more about **how** something was done. Remember, although adverbs of manner are usually connected to the verb, they can also modify the meaning of adjectives and other adverbs.

■ ADVERBS OF DEGREE

- Adverbs of degree also modify the meaning of verbs, adjectives and other adverbs. They tell us more about the **degree** to which an action is performed:

> 'Star was so unco-operative,' claims producer.

> *Manager Says*
> *Team Was Very Unlucky*

> You are too, too much, darling

- Other adverbs of degree include:
  much   more   most   totally   immensely   partly   completely
  fairly   rather   utterly   exceedingly   exceptionally

■ ADVERBS OF TIME

- Adverbs of time tell us about the time of an action: when it was carried out, when it is to be carried out and how often.

The show is performed twice daily.

CUT TAXES NOW!

> Soon the money will begin to roll in.

Parcels sent by first-class mail will arrive tomorrow.

- You will notice from the last sentence that adverbs can sometimes start sentences. The **placing** of adverbs within sentences depends on the **emphasis** you want to give. Usually, it will be placed next to the verb, adjective or other adverb it modifies, but sometimes, for emphasis, it can be put at the beginning of a sentence.

■ ADVERBS OF PLACE

- Adverbs of place tell us **where** the action takes place. They are normally placed next to the verb they modify:

    Place the knife and fork <u>here</u> and the spoons <u>there</u>.
    Take the plates <u>away</u> and bring <u>in</u> the pudding.
    Put the cat <u>out</u>.

- Many of these words are also used as prepositions (see Section 6).

ADVERBS FOR ASKING QUESTIONS

- There are four words that are classed as **interrogative adverbs**:

    when   where   how   why

- They are **interrogative** because they help a **question** to be expressed:

    <u>How</u> did we get into this mess?
    <u>Why</u> can't we know the facts?
    <u>When</u> is the economy going to improve?
    <u>Where</u> is the nearest shopping centre?

DEFINITELY, MAYBE AND NOT

- A few adverbs express **emphasis**:

    It was <u>definitely</u> a goal.
    <u>Certainly</u> I want to attend the meeting.
    <u>Assuredly</u>, the policy will succeed.
    <u>Surely</u> you're not going to use those tactics.
    <u>Unfortunately</u>, the truth is somewhat different.

- Some adverbs express **doubt**:

    It could <u>possibly</u> rain.
    The team will <u>probably</u> win.
    <u>Maybe</u> we weren't prepared thoroughly enough.
    <u>Perhaps</u> the answer is quite simple.

- The adverb **not** expresses a negative:

    I do <u>not</u> know the answer.

✓ *Checkpoint B*

Read the following opening to a story. Pick out all the adverbs and list them under these headings: *manner*, *time*, *place*, *degree*, *interrogation*, *emphasis*, *doubt or negation*.

Every Fish Has Its Day

Slowly and certainly, the goldfish circled its glass prison.

Tim watched it intently. There wasn't very much to a goldfish's life, he thought sadly. Why did people persist in cruelly enclosing them in glass bowls? Unfortunately, he was one of those people. Perhaps they did not mind, but maybe they did.

He watched as the fish swam monotonously round his circular path. Daily, the fish was condemned to this routine. Surely he was a bored fish. But how could a fish be bored, Tim thought.

Soon he would have to feed it. He looked at it closely, his attention drawn magnetically to its size. Undoubtedly, the fish was much bigger than it used to be. Indeed, it was really surprisingly bigger. Staggeringly bigger.

What was happening? Surely this was the result of watching too many bad movies on television, but wasn't the goldfish staring at him malevolently? Now it was bumping against the side of the bowl. The bowl began to rock alarmingly. The fish was trying to break out. This was utterly incredible.

Now the bowl had toppled over. It landed heavily on the carpet, the water flooding everywhere. Suddenly, there was a flash of gold and the fish had him by the throat . . .

Activity 2

Continue the story of 'Every fish has its day', using as many adverbs of manner, time and degree as appropriate. In addition, try to use some adverbs of place, some interrogative adverbs and some adverbs of emphasis, doubt and negation.

COMPARING WITH ADVERBS

- In the section on adjectives, we looked at how they formed their comparative and superlative forms. Adverbs, too, can be used to **compare** two or more things:

  She played the game <u>more enthusiastically</u> than he did.
  She played the game <u>most enthusiastically</u> of all the players.
  He jumped <u>further</u> than the other competitor.
  He jumped <u>furthest</u> of all the competitors.

- When an adverb has two or more syllables, it forms its **comparative** by putting 'more' in front of it and its '**superlative**' by putting 'most' in front of it:

carelessly	more carelessly	most carelessly
dogmatically	more dogmatically	most dogmatically
reasonably	more reasonably	most reasonably

- Some irregular adverbs have one syllable. These usually add '-er' for the **comparative** and '-est' for the **superlative**:

fast	faster	fastest
hard	harder	hardest

- As with adjectives, there are some **irregular** adverbs that form their comparatives and superlatives in their own way:

well	better	best
little	less	least
much	more	most
badly	worse	worst

Activity 3

Create sentences with a similar meaning to the examples below, but using the comparative and superlative forms of the adverbs underlined in these examples:
a) She was <u>desperate</u> to succeed.
b) He dressed <u>elegantly</u> and <u>tastefully</u>.
c) The game gave <u>little</u> in the way of opportunity for him to shine.
d) The tenor sang <u>badly</u> on that particular occasion.
e) I feel <u>well</u> considering what I've been through.

SKILLCHECK Check these statements to assess what you have learned from this section. If you cannot honestly tick every statement, go back over the section.

❏ I understand the function of adverbs.

❏ I realise that adverbs can modify the meaning of verbs, adjectives and other adverbs.

❏ I can recognise the main types of adverbs.

❏ I know how different adverbs form their comparatives and superlatives and that some adverbs form theirs in an irregular way.

6
PREPOSITIONS
THOSE LITTLE WORDS
SHOW WHERE IT'S AT

- **Prepositions are usually very small words. They are difficult to define.**
- **Prepositions often tell us something about position, place or time.**
- **They come before a noun or pronoun.**
- **They relate or 'refer' that noun or pronoun to something else in the sentence.**
- **All of these signs have prepositions:**

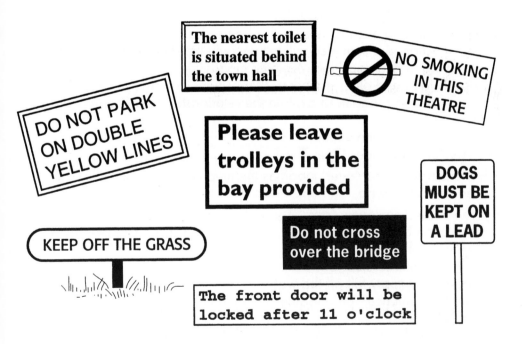

- The prepositions in these sentences are underlined:
    Gunman walks <u>into</u> bank, steals money <u>from</u> assistant, strolls <u>down</u> street
    Government Takes Advice <u>Of</u> Experts and Invests <u>In</u> Roads
    <u>After</u> the traffic lights, cross <u>over</u> the road and the hotel is <u>on</u> the left.

- These are the most common prepositions:

above	after	across	against	along	among	around	at
before	below	beneath	beside	between	beyond	by	
down	during						
for	from						
in							
near							
of	off	on	over				
since							
through							
under	underneath	until	up				
with	without						

- The word 'preposition' actually means 'place in front of'. A preposition shows the relation between the item it is placed in front of and some other word in the sentence:

    The fans rushed <u>through</u> the gates.

    The preposition 'through' shows the relation between 'gates' and 'fans'.

- Notice, too, that prepositions can come before **pronouns**:

    I waited <u>for</u> it for three hours.

    The whole thing was <u>beyond</u> him.

- Many of these prepositions can also be used as **adverbs** (see page 64). Their function in a sentence will tell you whether they are being used as an adverb or a preposition. Adverbs modify the meaning of verbs (as well as adjectives and other adverbs). Prepositions are always placed in front of a noun or a pronoun to explain the relationship between that word and some other word:

    'I fell <u>over</u>!' claims striker.

    Hamlet Actor Goes <u>Over</u> The Top

- In the first sentence, 'over' modifies the meaning of the verb 'fell'; it is used as an **adverb**.

- In the second sentence, 'over' comes before the noun 'top' and explains the relation between 'actor' and 'top'; it is used as an **preposition**.
    Here is another example:

    We told him to clear <u>off</u>.

    Humpty Dumpty fell <u>off</u> the wall.

    In the first sentence, 'off' modifies the meaning of 'clear' and is an **adverb**.

    In the second sentence, 'off' is placed in front of the noun 'wall' and explains the relation between it and 'Humpty Dumpty'; it is a **preposition**.

- Generally, prepositions tell us something about time and place.

    Dinner will be served <u>after</u> the speeches.

    The interval came <u>before</u> the main feature.

The prepositions 'after' and 'before' tell us **when** dinner will be served and what happened before the main feature was shown; they are **prepositions of time**.

    There is a promised land <u>beyond</u> the blue horizon.

    I do like to be <u>beside</u> the sea.

The prepositions 'beyond' and 'beside' tell us something about the place where the promised land is and where the 'I' of the sentence likes to be; they are **prepositions of place**.

✓ *Checkpoint A*

Read the following article and pick out all the prepositions. Be careful: there are some words used here as adverbs that can be used as prepositions in other contexts. Do not list these adverbs.

Peer in Angry Scuffle Outside the House of Lords

Lord Twitter, one of the richest aristocrats in the country, was involved in a violent argument with a passer-by as he left the House of Lords yesterday.

'This fellow was just walking past,' said Lord Twitter, 'when he shouted out something really disagreeable. No excuse for it, so I engaged him in an exchange of firm views.'

Spectators who happened to be nearby said that the peer had become incensed with anger and almost pushed the man though plate-glass windows.

The man, who refused to be named, claimed the peer's action was beneath contempt. On seeing Lord Twitter, he had hailed him in a friendly fashion only to be greeted by a volley of abuse in return.

'If this is the behaviour of our betters, then give me 'EastEnders' any day,' the man remarked.

In continuing to deny he was at fault, Lord Twitter reiterated his belief that he had been insulted. 'Insulted outside the House of Lords by a yob who happened to be passing by. What is this country coming to?'

In the past, Lord Twitter has been convicted of being drunk in possession of a motor vehicle and has several convictions for disturbing the peace. He is at present on probation for a year.

Activity 1

Read the following notice and fill in the gaps with an appropriate preposition.

CLEANLINESS IN THE PLAYGROUND

It is surely .... everybody's interest that our playground, ... the use .... which we are very grateful .... the education authority, should be kept .... good condition. .... doubt, this has not been the case despite all the complaints that have been made .... the schoolkeeping staff. .... the very least, pupils should be capable .... not dropping sweet papers and sandwich wrappings .... the ground. Please pay some attention .... this reminder and, ... all, do something .... it!

AVOIDING MISTAKES WITH PREPOSITIONS

People learning English as a second language frequently have difficulty in choosing the correct preposition for a particular phrase. You can only really become confident about prepositions through constant practice and awareness.

Activity 2

Read the following dialogue. Prepositions are misused throughout. Pick out these errors and replace each with the correct preposition.

JACK There's no doubt beyond it.

SUE What? What are you talking of?

JACK The warming at the planet. This planet is with a very serious condition.

SUE And you're on a position to know, I suppose.

JACK I'm backed with all the most important scientists from the world.

SUE You can't listen at them. Most from them are up the bend.

JACK That's a typically stupid statement. You have the courage by your ignorance. You know nothing between this earth you live at.

SUE Over your bike. Get from your hobby horse. Honestly, talk some sense.

JACK Having a conversation against you is next from impossible.

CHOOSING THE RIGHT PRONOUN

- When **prepositions** come in front of **pronouns**, you must be careful to choose the right form of the pronoun (see page 28).
- After a preposition, the **object** form of the pronoun is always used.
  The personal pronouns are:
      I we you he she it they
  The object form of those pronouns are:
      me us you him her it them
- So, in these sentences the object forms of the pronouns are used because they come after a preposition:
  Between <u>you</u> and <u>me</u>, there's something to <u>it</u>.
  Don't give it to <u>her</u>.
  The whole thing is beyond <u>us</u>.
  The present they gave <u>them</u> was quite hideous.

Activity 3

Read the following dialogue. Pronouns are used incorrectly. Rewrite the passage correcting these errors.

'I said it was from you and I. That didn't make any difference to she. Her husband was there too and he asked if it really was from we. It was for they we did it, but it wasn't appreciated by they. Just think what they have done to you and I in the past. She can't see past he. Between you and I, I think she's trying to tell we something. Like she doesn't want to be friends with you and I any more. That's up to she, that's what I think.'

SKILLCHECK   Check these statements to assess what you have learned from this section. If you cannot honestly tick every statement, go back over the section.

- ❏ I can recognise the words that are used as prepositions.
- ❏ I understand that some words can be used as both prepositions and adverbs, depending on their function within a sentence.
- ❏ I understand that the object form of pronouns should be used after prepositions.

6

7

CONJUNCTIONS
AND
INTERJECTIONS

- **A conjunction is a word used to join two things together.**
- **A conjunction can be used to join words:**
     fish <u>and</u> chips   tea <u>or</u> coffee
- **A conjunction can be used to join phrases (a phrase is a group of words without a finite verb):**
     your money <u>or</u> your life
- **A conjunction can be used to join clauses (a clause has a finite verb and a subject, and may nor may not be a sentence on its own).**
     <u>Before</u> you park your car please obtain a ticket from the machine.
- **A conjunction can be used to build a longer sentence from shorter sentences.**
     I disliked him intensely <u>and</u> did not want his favours, <u>but</u> I was desperate.

BUILDING SENTENCES

Conjunctions, also called **connectives**, are very important words, especially for the purpose of writing longer and more complex sentences (see Section 8).

- The most common conjunctions that are used to join words, phrases or sentences together are:
     and   or   but   neither   before   after   until   when
Here are some examples:
     That's <u>neither</u> here <u>nor</u> there.
     Slowly <u>but</u> surely, the snail advanced up the cabbage leaf.

✓ *Checkpoint A*

Read the following advertisement for a new film.
List the connectives used.

Excitement AND Terror!

Thrill to the new movie sensation and laugh, cry or love with these larger-than-life characters!

It was him or her! A fight to the death or a struggle to love! You might wait around for a greater movie than this, but you'll wait for a long, long time!

You may have thought Al Bandido was a star, until you saw him in

THE GODSON

After you have seen this movie, you'll think he is a superstar! You may have thought Michelle Piffle was great, before you saw her in

THE GODSON

When you have seen 'The Godson', you'll think she is the greatest!

▪ MORE ABOUT CONJUNCTIONS

Other very common conjunctions or connectives are:

although	as	since	so	so that
because		than	that	though	till
if	in order that	unless		
nor		whereas	while	whilst
provided that		yet		

WITHOUT US CONJUNCTIONS, YOU'D JUST BE A BUNCH OF SIMPLE SENTENCES

SINCE THAN AFTER SO BECAUSE YET AS THAT WHILE IF UNTIL

Read this extract from a letter and notice how conjunctions are used:

Dear Madam

<u>Although</u> we expect payment by the first of the month, we usually allow customers eight days' grace. <u>After</u> that period has elapsed, we usually have to institute proceedings, <u>as</u> we have to take into account our cashflow. However, <u>because</u> you are such an old and trusted customer, <u>and before</u> we took such a step in your case, we decided to delay, <u>if</u> you communicated with us immediately.

   <u>Since</u> we sent you our previous letter which explained the position, we have received no response from you, <u>though</u> we followed our letter with a telephone call. <u>Until</u> we had that conversation with you, we had no knowledge of the difficulties you were experiencing. <u>Unless</u> we know the facts, we cannot help our customers through temporary problems, <u>whereas</u> we now have been informed of your position <u>and</u> we can make arrangements to ease the burden of payment.

   We hasten to add <u>that</u>, <u>whilst</u> we are sympathetic to customers' problems, we also have our own financial obligations.

   We look forward to hearing from you.

Yours faithfully

M. Card.

M. Card

Most of the connectives listed above have been used in this letter.

- All of them have been used to link a **subordinate clause** of the sentence to the **main clause**.

– A **clause** has a **finite verb**. This is a verb that has a **subject**, although the subject may not always be stated. So, in the clause 'Stop!' it is understood that the subject is 'you' and the meaning is *'You must stop!'*.
– A **main clause** is a clause that can be a sentence by itself. Every sentence has to have at least one main clause.
– A **subordinate clause** is a clause that cannot be a sentence by itself: until we arrive   as you know   because I want to

- A conjunction or connective is often used to link a subordinate clause to a main clause.
- Conjunctions are extremely useful tools in helping you to write longer, more complex and more interesting sentences.
Consider this passage from a story, for example. No connectives have been used.

> He had missed her. She had walked out three weeks previously. They had quarrelled badly. Now he wanted to make it up with her. How could she do that? It had been such a bad parting of the ways. It had seemed like the end of their relationship.
> He arranged to meet her. He arrived at the restaurant. They usually ate there. She had not arrived. He was shown to the table. He waited anxiously. Minutes went by. A half-hour went by. He knew. She wasn't going to come.
> He saw her. She was hesitating at the entrance to the room. She was looking round. She was obviously searching for his face. He smiled. She smiled back. All was well again. They had a chance now.

The story is a succession of short sentences – a pattern which becomes repetitive and uninteresting. Connectives could make the writing less repetitive and more interesting for your reader:

> He had missed her since she had walked out three weeks previously. Although they had quarrelled badly, he now wanted to make it up. How could she do that? Since it had been such a bad parting of the ways it had seemed like the end of their relationship.
> He arranged to meet her. When he arrived at the restaurant where they usually ate, he was shown to the table. He waited anxiously. Minutes and then half an hour went by. He knew she wasn't going to come.
> Then he saw her. She was hesitating at the entrance to the room, looking around, obviously searching for his face. He smiled, so she smiled back. They now had a chance so all was well again.

In this version, longer sentences, formed with the help of **connectives**, combine with short sentences to make a more fluent and interesting piece of story-telling.

- In your own writing, you should aim to use conjunctions to create longer, more complex sentences when it is appropriate to do so.

CONJUNCTIONS AND INTERJECTIONS

Activities 1 and 2

1 Read the following letter and then rewrite it using conjunctions, and making small changes where appropriate, to cut down the number of separate, short sentences and make longer, more complex sentences.

> Dear Sir
>
> It gives us great pleasure to write to inform you of some good news. You have won a prize in our lottery. You are a valued customer. Your name was entered into our draw last month. The lucky numbers were chosen. You are one of the fortunate prize-winners.
>
> You want to receive this valuable prize. You must take these steps. Send in three thousand packet tops of our cereal 'Teethcracker'. We will send you the cash prize. This offer remains open until June 25th of this year. We do not hear from you, the cash prize will be forfeit.
>
> Yours faithfully
>
> *a. Gradgrind*
>
> A. Gradgrind

2 Read the opening to this short story. It has been written in a succession of short, simple sentences. It could be improved by the use of conjunctions, reducing the number of sentences by making longer, more complex sentences. To do this you might want to make other small changes.

ALIEN

It had come from another world. It had travelled through space. It had travelled in a spacecraft. It could go faster than the speed of light.

Its masters had realised something. The alien would be conspicuous in Dorking High Street. The bug eyes, the 24 feet and the light that flashed on top of its head would attract attention. They had devised an instant camouflage.

There was one problem. The disguise chosen looked just like the Prime Minister!

It walked down Dorking High Street. People stared at it. The humans came up to it. They seized its hand. It wondered why. It had been instructed how to deal with some eventualities. This was different. It was only five minutes after its landing on earth. People were asking for its autograph. They seemed to know it.

INTERJECTIONS – EXPRESSING A REACTION

- What are **interjections**? They are the words (usually quite short words) that express some sudden emotion such as surprise, disgust, excitement, regret, doubt, certainty or triumph.

  Some of the more common interjections are:

well!	ah!	oh!	really!	ouch!	oh dear!	hey!	what a pity!	hello!
			never!	wow!	rubbish!	of course!		

- Notice that interjections are often single words but they may also be in the form of a **phrase**:

  what a surprise!   now then!

- You will also have noticed that **exclamation marks** have been used after these interjections. If they stand on their own (and they may do so), it is usual to place exclamation marks after them for emphasis. If they come at the beginning of the sentence, then the exclamation mark may come at the end of the sentence:

Phew! What A Scorcher!

Well, that'll be the day!

- In more formal writing, you will not normally use interjections. If you are using direct speech or writing informally, however, you may use them, although if they are used often they may have less impact.

Activity 3

Read the following dialogue. Gaps have been left which you should fill with an appropriate interjection (word or phrase). Answers have been suggested at the back, but be creative here.

ADA   ...., I never!

JOHN   ...., what are you going on about now?

ADA   ...., you could have knocked me down with a feather! They've split up!

JOHN   ....!

ADA   ...., I never thought that would happen!

JOHN   ....!

ADA   ....!

JOHN   ....! What do you expect? The world's gone mad these days! Nothing's sacred.

ADA   ....! ...., it is!

SKILLCHECK   Check these statements to assess what you have learned from this section. If you cannot honestly tick every statement, go back over the section.

❑ I understand the function of conjunctions in sentences.

❑ I realise that I may use conjunctions to write longer, more varied sentences in my own writing.

❑ I know what interjections are and how to punctuate them.

8
MORE ABOUT SENTENCES

- **The rules of grammar enable us to join words and make sentences.**
- **Sentences are the units you use to build up a piece of writing.**
- **To be a sentence, a word or a group of words must make sense standing on its own.**
- **A sentence always begins with a capital letter.**
- **A sentence must have a full stop, a question mark or an exclamation mark at the end.**
- **A sentence must have at least one verb.**

- When you are **writing** in English, you are usually required to write in **complete sentences**:

    There will be a general election on June the sixth.

    In **speech**, it is quite usual to use **incomplete sentences**. For example, if you were asked when the general election will take place, you might well answer:

On June
the sixth.

It is understood that this incomplete sentence stands in for:

    The general election will take place on June the sixth.

In speech, this would be an unnecessary repetition. Incomplete sentences like the one above are acceptable because it is clear what is meant.

When you use direct speech in your writing, in narrative or personal writing, you will be able to use incomplete sentences when you are putting down the actual words someone says.

In most of your writing, however, you will have to use complete sentences. We have already looked at what constitutes a complete sentence in the sections on nouns, verbs and conjunctions.

Here are some reminders about what a sentence consists of.
    Stop!

- This is a complete sentence, because it is giving an order. It makes sense on its own. It has a finite verb and the subject is understood (*you* stop).

- A sentence may consist of one word, if that word is a finite verb with a subject that is understood. Most one-word sentences are of this type: **imperatives** (giving an order). Other examples would be:
    Pray.   Sit.   Fetch.   Eat.

- There are occasions when, in writing as well as in speech, a response to a question or some kind of affirmative or negative statement takes the form of one word:
    Yes.   No.   Certainly.   Happy birthday.

- These do not contain a finite verb and cannot be described as sentences, but they can usefully be thought of as **sentence-equivalents**, because it is understood what the surrounding words would be if they were written out in full.

- In your own writing, however, you must be absolutely sure about when you are writing in complete sentences. The following examples are all phrases because they have **no subject** and **no finite verb**:
    about the house.
    round the bend.
    in the cottage.
    for four years.
These are **phrases**. They might be used in speech as responses to questions, but they are not sentences because **they do not make sense on their own**.

- These are sentences, however, because with the addition of a subject and a finite verb, they do make sense on their own:
    He never tired of talking about the house.
    They're driving me round the bend.
    She spent a week in the cottage.
    I attended that college for four years.

Read the following advertisement. Make two lists under the headings:
Complete sentences and *Incomplete sentences*.

IN THE RED

Usually, it's not done to be in the red.

But when the red is the laser red colour of
the Gaudy Élite 80, then who wouldn't be in the red?
Hardly anyone.

An electric twenty-first century red. A stylish, sensual
red. Not your ordinary red of a football shirt.
But the red of an élite. A Gaudy Élite.

And the performance isn't that bad either. Top speed
of 125 m.p.h. Power-assisted steering. Sun-roof.
Automatic gears. It's touches like these that make
driving pleasurable.

Get in the red. Your bank manager won't even mind.
But she will notice.

8

SENTENCES

Activity 1

Make each of the phrases below into a complete sentence by adding a subject
and a finite verb.

a) once again
b) forever and ever
c) in the park
d) the parents
e) in a fierce argument

SIMPLE SENTENCES – SAYING ONE THING

- A simple sentence makes one statement, issues one instruction or asks one question. These are all examples of simple sentences:

Just do it

We appreciate your co-operation in refraining from smoking

Do you support the testing of new medical drugs on animals?

- A simple sentence has one finite verb.
- A simple sentence has one subject.
- A simple sentence makes one statement.
- A simple sentence consists of one main clause.
- The three sentences above are examples of simple sentences. This sentence is another example.

■ FOUR MAIN TYPES OF SIMPLE SENTENCES

Type 1
The subject **is** something. Thus, type 1 simple sentences always contain the verb 'to be'. For example:
> They <u>were</u> absolutely furious.
> The player <u>was</u> as sick as the proverbial parrot.
> The game <u>is</u> up.
> The elephant <u>is</u> a basically gentle creature.

- If these sentences are turned into **questions**, the word order is changed but the structure is the same: subject + a form of the verb 'to be':
> Were they absolutely furious?
> Was the player as sick as a parrot?
> Is the game up?
> Is the elephant a basically gentle creature?

Type 2
The subject of the sentence **does** something. The verbs in this type of simple sentence are **intransitive**. That means they do not take an object, though they may have an adverb which describes how the action is done.
> a) She laughed.
> b) She laughed loudly.
> c) The birds fell to the ground.
> d) The criminal disagreed with the verdict.
> e) The class behaved atrociously.

In (b) and (e) 'loudly' and 'atrociously' are adverbs. In (c) 'to the ground' is an adverbial phrase attached to the intransitive verb 'fell'. In (d) 'with the verdict' is an adverbial phrase attached to the intransitive verb 'behaved'.

- In type 2 of the simple sentence, there is a someone or something that performs the action and there is the action itself.

Type 3

There is a **subject**, a **finite verb** and an **object**.

Someone or something does something to someone or something.

All the verbs in this type of simple sentence are **transitive**, that is, they take an object.

Type 3 simple sentences may also have an adverb or adverbial phrase which describes how the action is done. For example:

The songwriter composed the song in a matter of minutes.

The golfer hit the ball into the far distance.

They recognised one another immediately.

They baked several loaves of bread.

Type 4

The subject of the sentence 'appears to be', 'seems', 'becomes', 'feels', or 'looks' (*like* not *at*):

The family appears to be happy.

The argument seems to be without fault.

The weather became even worse.

I felt absolutely terrible.

It looks like curtains for him.

The verbs <u>appear</u>, <u>become</u>, <u>seem</u>, <u>feel</u>, <u>look</u> are the verbs most often used in this type of simple sentence. They are usually followed by the verb 'to be' and/or an adjective or adverb.

✓ *Checkpoint B*

The following opening to a story consists entirely of simple sentences. List each under the appropriate heading of type 1, 2, 3 or 4 of simple sentence as described in the section above.

The bank was in the middle of Main Street. The getaway car glided to a halt near it. Everything appeared normal. Shoppers went about their business. There was the usual quota of loungers. No one paid any attention to the nondescript vehicle.

The two men in the back seat got out of the car. The driver left the engine running. The men seemed to be without a care in the world. They looked around. Then they walked the few yards to the door of the bank.

It was not particularly busy inside the bank. There were a few people waiting for the tellers. The men joined a short queue. They seemed to be waiting patiently for their turn.

The queue shortened. Then it was their turn. Suddenly, the men pulled stockings out of their pockets. They pulled them over their faces. These were bank robbers. Now they were brandishing guns. They issued instructions rapidly and gruffly.

Activity 2

Continue the above story as you wish, but use simple sentences only, varying the type you use according to the four types described in the section above.

COMPOUND OR DOUBLE SENTENCES – LINKING TWO THINGS

a)

> Please take a seat and a waitress will take your order

b)

> *Patrons should hold on to their ticket stubs and order their interval drinks before the performance.*

- The above are examples of **compound** or **double sentences**.
- They consist of **two main clauses**, each of **equal importance** and each having a **subject** and a **finite verb**.
- Neither clause is dependent on the other. They are joined by the **connective** 'and'. Each example could have been written as two separate sentences, but by joining them together, the writer has made a **connection** between the two statements.
- Notice that in (b) 'patrons' is the subject of both sentences, but it has been omitted from the second because that would involve unnecessary repetition.
- As explained on page 72, other connectives (also called conjunctions) that can be used to join two simple sentences include:

or	nor	but	yet

Further examples:
> You can pay the entire bill now, <u>or</u> you can pay by instalments.
> <u>Neither</u> is she a good sport, <u>nor</u> is she amusing.
> The club could have survived, <u>but</u> there was no money left.
> He seemed pleasant enough, <u>yet</u> there was something about him that disturbed her.

In your own writing do not overdo the joining of simple sentences by 'and', as it tends to become monotonous.

MULTIPLE SENTENCES – THREE OR MORE SIMPLE THINGS

- A compound or double sentence consists of two simple sentences joined by a conjunction.

> DON'T TRY AND THREATEN ME WITH YOUR COMPOUND AND MULTIPLE SENTENCES!

- A multiple sentence consists of **three or more simple sentences** joined by conjunctions:
    The umpires left the pavilion <u>and</u> inspected the pitch, <u>but</u> the rain continued to fall.
    Be quick <u>and</u> finish your breakfast <u>or</u> you'll be late for school.
    The postman rang the bell, received no answer <u>and</u> left the parcel outside the door.

- Notice that in the last example all three sentences within the multiple sentence have the **same subject**: the postman. One of the conjunctions has been left out. The three sentences could have been written as three separate sentences like this:
    The postman rang the bell. The postman received no answer. The postman left the parcel outside the door.
This is unnecessarily repetitive, even if the pronoun 'he' had been substituted for 'postman' in the second and third sentences. Written as a multiple sentence, the **comma** after the first sentence acts like a conjunction and then 'and' joins the second and third sentences.

✓ Checkpoint C

Read the following article. Identify each of the sentences as being either a simple, compound or multiple sentence.

The popularity of television soap operas never seems to wane. 'Coronation Street', 'EastEnders' and 'Brookside' have been running for years now and audiences in their millions continue to watch them.

The fascination of soaps has to do with familiarity. Audiences identify with the characters, make them their 'friends' and live their lives with them. Most soap actors are totally identified with their characters and are scarcely known by their own names. Some actors do not mind this, but others resent it. They enjoy the fame, they have the security of a long-running television series, but they lose their identity to their fictional character.

Viewers regularly send letters to 'Emmerdale' or write to 'EastEnders' characters with advice. For many people, these soap characters are real people. Perhaps these fanatics lack something in their own lives, or want to lose themselves in a fictional world. Escapism is an integral part of soap operas, but it can be dangerous and people can avoid facing up to their own problems. The characters of the soaps are only imitation people, but try telling that to the millions of fans.

8

SENTENCES

Activity 3

Rewrite the following sentences as either compound or multiple sentences.
- **a)** She lost her purse. She reported it to the police.
- **b)** The father cooked the meal. He called the children to the table. They did not come.
- **c)** The DJ played the song. He repeated it by general request. He refused to play it a third time.
- **d)** The car picked up speed. It passed the slow-moving lorry.
- **e)** He tried to study. He found it boring. He packed it in.

COMPLEX SENTENCES – SPOTTING THE MAIN CLAUSE

LET ME REMIND YOU SUBORDINATES I'M THE MAIN CLAUSE AND YOU'RE DEPENDENT ON ME!

- A **complex sentence** consists of one **main clause** and one or more **subordinate** or **dependent clauses**.

- The **main clause** in a complex sentence is like a **simple sentence** within a complex sentence. The main clause is the sentence round which the rest of the sentence is built. Here are some examples of complex sentences.

  | Do not open the door | until the train comes to a stop. |
  | *main clause* | *subordinate clause* |

  The main clause is 'Do not open the door'.
  The subordinate or dependent clause is 'until the train comes to a stop'.

  | Passengers are advised | that they must have a valid ticket | |
  | *main clause* | *subordinate clause* | |

  before they board the train.
  subordinate clause

- In this second example, there is a main clause and two subordinate clauses.
  The main clause is 'Passengers are advised'. The two subordinate or dependent clauses are 'that they must have a valid ticket' and 'before they board the train'.

- Remember that a **clause** must have a **subject** and a **finite verb**.
- The main clause of a complex sentence need not come at the beginning of the sentence, as in this example:

    Although every effort is made to ensure the security of passengers' luggage, <u>passengers are advised to use identification labels</u> in order that mistakes can be avoided.

    The main clause in this sentence has one subordinate clause before it and another after it.

    Sometimes the main clause of a complex sentence can be retained till the very end of a long sentence after several subordinate clauses:

    When the train arrives at King's Cross, if passengers intend to continue their journey beyond London and have to catch a train at another London terminal, <u>they are advised to contact the station manager's office.</u>

- When you are writing complex sentences, identify your main clause and use this as the building block on which to construct the rest of the sentence.

✓ Checkpoint D

Read the following set of instructions about how to make a pot of tea. Each sentence is a complex sentence. Pick out the main clause in every sentence.

- When the water in the kettle is boiling, pour some of it into the teapot.
- After you rinse the pot thoroughly, put one teaspoon of tea in the pot for each person.
- Pour the boiling water into the pot, until it is as full as you wish, before you cover the pot with a tea-cosy.
- The tea should infuse for at least five minutes so that it is full of flavour when it is poured.

8

SENTENCES

Activity 4

Join the following groups of sentences into one complex sentence.
   a) The animal hid under the bed all day. It was very upset. It missed its former home.
   b) The radio was blaring. The neighbours complained. The workmen had to turn it off.
   c) She returned from the city by five. He met her at the station. They went to the cinema.
   d) Saturday was his favourite day. He could get up late. He could do some shopping. He could do some of his favourite things.

SUBORDINATE CLAUSES – DEPENDING ON A SIMPLE SENTENCE

A subordinate clause is a clause (it has a verb and a subject) that cannot be a sentence by itself:

until we arrive   as you know   because I want to

There are three types of subordinate clause: adjectival, adverbial and noun clauses.

■ ADJECTIVAL CLAUSES

- **Adjectival clauses** must have a finite verb and describe a noun, pronoun or noun equivalent in the main clause of the sentence.
- Adjectival clauses are often joined to the main clause by relative pronouns:

who   whom   whose   which   that

Sometimes they are linked by conjunctions:

where   when   why   as

when they are used to introduce a clause that is describing a noun or pronoun.

The toilets, <u>which are situated on the fifth floor</u>, are for the use of the store's customers only.

The underlined words make up an adjectival clause describing (or 'qualifying') the word 'toilets'. The adjectival clause is joined to the main clause (which is divided) by the relative pronoun 'which'.

The staff welfare officer, <u>whose office is in the main annexe</u>, is available to give advice between the hours of 10 a.m. and 5 p.m..

The underlined words comprise an adjectival clause with the relative pronoun 'whose' describing 'officer'.

This plaque marks the exact spot <u>where the allied troops landed on D-Day.</u>

Although the underlined clause in this sentence is introduced by the **conjunction** 'where', it is an adjectival clause describing 'spot'.

- Very often in English the relative pronoun joining an adjectival clause to the main clause of a sentence is left out. It becomes understood:

Prague is the city <u>the whole world wants to visit</u>.

The underlined words above are an adjectival clause where the relative pronoun 'that' or 'which' has been omitted.

The Old Town Square is the place <u>most tourists head for</u>.

In this sentence, the underlined words make up another adjectival clause where 'where', 'that' or 'which' has been left out.

✓ *Checkpoint E*

Read this extract from a holiday brochure and pick out the adjectival clauses in each sentence.

> Prague has an international flavour which it is difficult to match. In the new Czech Republic, which has only been in existence for a few years, Prague is the centre of government, business and culture. It is the place where business people from all over the world converge. It is the cultural centre that has few equals. It is a city whose population has been through good times and bad times. It prefers the good times when the Czech wine flows and Czech fine cuisine flourishes.

Activity 5

Write a short entry for a holiday brochure praising the attractions of a location you know well and using an adjectival clause in every sentence.

■ ADVERBIAL CLAUSES

- Adverbial clauses are also **subordinate** or dependent clauses. They are dependent on the main clause of a sentence and qualify the meaning of the verb in that main clause.
- Adverbial clauses are of various types.
- There are adverbial clauses of **time**:
    The time of arrival will be announced <u>when that information becomes available</u>.
  The underlined words make up an adverbial clause of time. The adverbial clause qualifies the meaning of the verb in the main clause 'will be announced'. It tells us the time when the information will be announced.
- Adverbial clauses of time are usually joined to the main clause by these conjunctions:
    when   before   until   as   as soon as   after   since
  Here is another example of an adverbial clause of time:
    <u>Before you park your car</u> please obtain a ticket from the machine.
  The underlined words are an adverbial clause of time qualifying the meaning of the verb 'obtain' in the main clause of the sentence.

- There are also adverbial clauses of **place**. An adverbial clause of place tells us **where** the action of the verb in the main clause takes place.
  Please sign the document <u>where it is indicated</u> you should do so.
  The underlined words are an adverbial clause of place, qualifying the meaning of the verb 'sign' in the main clause of the sentence.
- Conjunctions used to join adverbial clauses of place to the main clause are usually 'where' or 'wherever':
  <u>Wherever you may roam</u>, there's no place like home.
  Please inform the customs <u>where you have been travelling</u>.
- There are also adverbial clauses of **reason**. They tell us the reason why something was done.
  Customers are advised to secure their cars <u>because thieves are known to operate in this car park</u>.
  The underlined words are an adverbial clause of reason; they qualify the verb advised in the main clause.
- Adverbial clauses of reason are often introduced by the conjunctions
  because   as   since   whereas   for   why
  'Since' and 'as' can introduce adverbial clauses of time and of reason. If you think about what they mean, you will be able to identify which type they are.
  Check your change, <u>as mistakes cannot be rectified later</u>.
  <u>Since the concert has been cancelled</u>, there will be a refund on tickets already purchased.

✓ *Checkpoint F*

Read the following speech and identify the adverbial clauses under the headings: *Time, Place* and *Reason*.

'I hope that, when we review the school year, we will have made progress. Where we haven't been doing so well, I am sure we can improve. We will improve because all of us want to do well. When exam time comes around again, we will all feel pressure, as naturally it is an important phase. Because we will have prepared well, I am sure we will all do ourselves credit. Then there is the issue of the new sports field. It is important it is situated where it is convenient for staff and pupils. When the time comes to make a decision, all of you will be consulted, as this is clearly a very important matter for the school.'

Activity 6

Write a mini-story with the title 'The Night Visitor' using adverbial clauses of time, place and reason wherever appropriate.

■ MORE ABOUT ADVERBIAL CLAUSES

- Other types of adverbial clauses are:

> manner   comparison *or* degree   purpose   result   condition
>   concession

- Adverbial clauses of **manner** usually employ the conjunctions 'how' or 'as':

    Employees are informed that bonuses reflect <u>how productivity has been maintained during the previous month</u>.

    The underlined words are an adverbial clause of manner qualifying the verb reflect. It tells us in what manner 'the bonuses reflect'.

- Adverbial clauses of **comparison** or **degree** usually have the conjunctions 'than' or 'as' joining them to the main clause of the sentence:

    Customers may withdraw as much <u>as they wish</u>.

    In this sentence, the adverbial clause of degree (the underlined words) qualifies the adverb 'much' rather than the verb of the clause, but it is still an adverbial clause. It tells us the degree to which customers can withdraw money.

    Journeys may take longer <u>than is usual on this route</u> because of engineering works.

    The underlined words are an adverbial clause of comparison. It makes a comparison between two things.

- Adverbial clauses can also indicate the **purpose** of something, the purpose behind the action described in the verb in the main clause of a sentence. The conjunctions

    that   so that   in order that   in case

    are used to join this type of adverbial clause to the main clause of a sentence:

    This section of the restaurant has been closed <u>in order that it can be cleaned</u>.

    Please have the correct money ready <u>so that delays can be avoided</u>.

- Adverbial clauses of **result** are usually introduced by 'so that' or 'that'.

    The company regretfully announces that business has decreased substantially <u>so that redundancies are inevitable</u>.

- Adverbial clauses of **condition** explain the conditions under which something will, or will not, be done. The conjunctions usually employed are 'if' and 'unless'.

    British Air announces that all flights are cancelled for today, <u>unless weather conditions improve</u>.

    <u>If a red light shows on the dashboard</u>, switch off the engine immediately.

- Adverbial clauses of **concession** express something that is granted or conceded. They are usually introduced by 'though', 'although' and 'even though'.

Although the company accepts no responsibility for the delay, it has been decided as a gesture of goodwill to compensate passengers. Latecomers cannot be admitted to the auditorium, though every effort will be made to find a suitable interval for them to take their seats.

✓ Checkpoint G

Read the following letter and list adverbial clauses of manner, comparison, degree, purpose, result, condition and concession.

Dear Jerry,

You have no idea how good I feel about passing my test. Although I started learning to drive with great hopes of success, I thought that I might have to try the test two or three times, so I was prepared to be disappointed. I can't imagine that anyone took it more seriously than I have done. If you have any doubts yourself about taking the test, let me know so I can give you some tips.

In order that we can catch up with things, I suggest we meet soon. Let's arrange a time and a place so that it's convenient for us both. I would imagine you'll want to hear all the latest gossip just as much as I do.

If I don't hear from you in the next week, I will contact you again, though please try to ring me. Let's make some definite arrangements so we can meet up.

Best wishes,

Ray

Activity 7

Write a letter complaining about the quality of some item you bought by mail order. You should use adverbial clauses of manner, comparison, degree, purpose, result, condition or concession wherever appropriate.

∎ NOUN CLAUSES

- **Noun clauses** perform the **function of a noun** but as a subordinate clause to the main clause of the sentence.

    London Transport informs passengers <u>that fares will be increased from September 1st</u>.

    The safety of passengers is <u>what is most important to this airline</u>.

    In the sentences the underlined words are noun clauses introduced by the conjunctions 'that' and 'what'.

- **Noun clauses** can also come at the beginning of sentences and perform the function of being the **subject** of the verb in the main clause.
  <u>What will happen in the future</u> remains a mystery.
  The underlined words form a noun clause which acts as the subject of the verb 'remains'.
- Noun clauses are often used in **indirect questions**:
  He asked him <u>what he knew about the accident</u>.
- Although many noun clauses have 'that' or 'what' as the joining word frequently, 'that' is omitted in front of a noun clause:
  The government announced <u>it is going to raise taxes</u>.
  The 'that' has been left out in this sentence, but the underlined words still make up a noun clause. One useful way of recognising a noun clause is by asking yourself whether '**something**' could replace the noun clause and still make sense:
  The authorities have granted her <u>what she asked for</u>.
  The authorities have granted her <u>something</u>.
  The newspapers questioned <u>what the real truth of the situation was</u>.
  The newspapers questioned <u>something</u>.
- Remember, if there is no finite verb, there is no clause.

✓ Checkpoint H

Read the following official notice and pick out the noun clauses that have been used in it.

> Your local council has decided that council charges will have to be increased significantly from April next year. What has not yet been decided is the rate of increase that is to be imposed. That it will be substantial is beyond doubt.
>
> The council considers the policies of central government to be responsible for this increase. We believe that this government is not interested in providing decent local services. It has decided that funds previously provided to subsidise local services will be severely reduced. We have continually queried what the government is up to, but we regret to say that our voice has been ignored.
>
> Households will be informed of the new rate when the decision is taken. This is a preliminary announcement to warn local people what lies in store. We do not take responsibility for what central government has instigated.

8

SENTENCES

8

SENTENCES

9
COMMON
GRAMMATICAL
ERRORS

SUBJECT–VERB AGREEMENT

We have already dealt with subject–verb agreement in Section 3, but there are a number of other points that need to be emphasised about this important matter of grammar.

- As we have learnt already, a **singular subject** requires a verb in the **singular** form and a **plural subject** requires a verb in the **plural** form. It is, however, sometimes not easy to tell whether you have a singular or a plural subject.
  For example, this kind of subject might lead you to think that you have a plural subject:
  One of our ships <u>has</u> gone missing.
  As the word 'ships' is next to the verb you might think that you need a plural verb (have), but in fact the **subject** of the sentence is 'one', which takes a singular verb.
  Here is another example of a similar kind:
  A selection of desserts is displayed for the convenience of the customers.
  The **subject** is the collective noun 'selection', not the plural 'desserts', so the verb has to be singular.
- The subject of a verb can be placed after the verb and this can sometimes lead to confusion about subject–verb agreement:
  Down in the valley are numerous isolated farms.
  The subject of the sentence is 'farms', not the singular 'valley', so this sentence requires a plural verb.

▪ COMPOUND SUBJECTS

- If the subject of a sentence consists of two or more singular nouns or pronouns, or a singular noun and a singular pronoun, joined by 'and', then there must be a **plural verb**:

    Mother <u>and</u> baby <u>are</u> both doing well.
    She <u>and</u> I <u>are</u> sworn enemies.
    You <u>and</u> that dog <u>are</u> inseparable.

Activity 1

Read the following advertisement. There are several mistakes of subject–verb agreement. Pick these out and rewrite the advertisement with the correct agreements.

ONLY **ONE** OF US IS TOPS

A huge range of personal CD players are available to you, the discriminating music-lover.

Round every street corner exists enticing ads telling you about yet another brilliant CD player.

The problems a teenager has to face up to! Hasn't you all enough problems? But you and your mates loves your music.

The choice and the solution is easy.
Boni is the CD player for you.

Across the globe more Boni CD players is bought than any other brand.

You and Boni possesses the secret. We're simply the **tops**.

COUNTABLE AND UNCOUNTABLE NOUNS

- Some common errors can be avoided by asking yourself whether a noun is 'countable' or 'uncountable'.
- Countable nouns have a singular and a plural form:
    one apple   two apples   two days   one day
    50 million people   1 person
- Uncountable nouns have a singular form only:
    water   violence   leather   some information.

- Uncountable nouns can often be made into countable units:
    a glass of water   an act of violence   a piece of information.
- **'Some'** is used with both countable and uncountable nouns, but it is used with the **singular** form of uncountable nouns (their only form) and the plural of **countable** nouns:
    some water   some glasses of water.
- **'Many'**, **'a few'** and **'few'** are used with countable nouns:
    many books   a few children   few ideas ('meaning not many').
- **'Much'**, **'a little'** and **'little'** (quantity, not size) are used with uncountable nouns:
    much time   a little wine (meaning 'some wine')   little hope (meaning 'not much').
- A mistake which is often heard is the confusion of **'less'** and **'fewer'**. 'Fewer' refers to countable nouns, less to uncountable nouns.
    fewer rolls   fewer swear words   fewer facts
    less cheese   less swearing   less knowledge
The most common mistake of all is 'less people'. It should always be 'fewer people'. Think about it: 'people' is a plural so the noun must be countable.

Activity 2

There are some errors in the use of much/many and less/fewer in this passage. Rewrite the passage correcting these errors.

Much has been made of the many difficulties of learning to be computer literate, but there are less problems than much people claim. It is true that much difficulties have to be put up with in the much initial attempts to master a computer, but many fewer than usually predicted. Less people than you would expect have many trouble with learning this important new skill.

MIXING UP PRONOUNS

- You have to be very careful when using pronouns that it is absolutely clear to what or to whom they refer.
    For example, in this sentence there is confusion about what the pronoun 'it' refers to:
        When the cat brushed against the dog, <u>it</u> froze with fear.
    The cat or the dog froze with fear? This sentence would be clearer expressed like this:
        When the cat brushed against <u>it</u>, the dog froze with fear.
    Another example:
        When the bookmakers paid the punters their winnings, <u>they</u> were less than delighted.

Who were less than delighted – the bookmakers or the punters? The sentence could have been expressed like this:

When the bookmakers paid <u>them</u> their winnings, <u>the punters</u> were less than delighted.

When <u>they</u> paid the punters their winnings, <u>the bookmakers</u> were less than delighted.

- If you use a **singular noun** and then refer to the noun with a **pronoun** later, the pronoun must '**agree**' with the noun:

    <u>A football player</u> has a short career; <u>they</u> can only stay at the top for about ten years.

In this sentence, 'football player' is singular; so 'they' is wrong. The sentence should read:

    <u>A football player</u> has a short career; <u>he</u> can only stay at the top for ten years.

Here is another example:

    <u>A leopard</u> is a very majestic creature. <u>They</u> are one of the most graceful animals in the world.

Here 'leopard' is singular and, therefore, the second sentence should read:

    <u>It</u> is one of the most graceful animals in the world.

- However, in everyday English, it is becoming common to use 'they' in the **singular** sense to avoid using the rather clumsy 'he/she', 'she/he' or even 's/he':

    When a <u>doctor</u> becomes fully qualified, <u>she/he</u> can set up in general practice.

The 'doctor' in this sentence may be female or male and this is indicated by the use of 'she/he'. To avoid this clumsy expression, you sometimes see:

    When <u>a doctor</u> becomes fully qualified, <u>they</u> can set up in general practice.

This is technically ungrammatical, but it is becoming accepted by usage.

- An alternative and better way of expressing this would be to make 'doctors' **plural**, then there is no difficulty about the gender of the pronoun:

    When <u>doctors</u> become fully qualified, <u>they</u> can set up in general practice.

UNATTACHED PHRASES

- A **participial phrase** begins with a present participle ending in '**-ing**' or a past participle, which usually ends in '**-ed**' (see Verbs, page 48). It affects the meaning of the subject **nearest** to it:

    <u>Having missed</u> the boat, <u>they</u> waited for the next one.
    <u>Making up</u> her mind suddenly, <u>she</u> decided to leave.
    <u>Having lost</u> a lot of money at the tables, <u>the gambler</u> left the casino.
    <u>Puzzled</u> by the confusion, <u>the detective</u> went over the evidence again.

- However, confusion occurs if the **nearest subject** is not the one which should be affected by the phrase with the participle.

> Having bow legs and an oval shape, <u>the dealer</u> liked the antique table.

This sentence implies that 'the dealer' had the bow legs and the oval shape. It would be better expressed like this:

> The dealer liked the antique table as it had bow legs and an oval shape.

Here are some other examples of incorrectly attached phrases:
> <u>Climbing</u> the mountain, <u>the snow</u> engulfed him.

This sentence could be rewritten by keeping the participle but relating it to the proper subject:
> <u>Climbing</u> the mountain, <u>he</u> was engulfed by the snow.
> <u>Entering</u> the palace, <u>the sound</u> of trumpets greeted the queen.

This could be rewritten in one of these two ways:
> <u>Entering</u> the palace, <u>the queen</u> was greeted by the sound of trumpets.

or
> As she entered the palace, the queen was greeted by the sound of trumpets.

- A phrase affecting the nearest subject may be introduced by something other than a participle.
> Before <u>visiting</u> his relatives, <u>he</u> bought some presents for them.
> Although <u>doubting</u> the soundness of the policy, the <u>politician</u> gave his approval to it.
> After <u>reviewing</u> the evidence, <u>the judge</u> refused the request for a retrial.

- Again, adjectival or adverbial phrases at the beginning of sentences need to be clearly attached to the subject that follows:
> Since <u>coming</u> to this town, <u>the population</u> has grown three times as large.

It is not 'the population' that has come to this town so the sentence is confusing. It needs to be rewritten:
> Since she came to this town, the population has grown three times as large.

Here is another example of a sentence with an unattached phrase:
> After <u>waiting</u> fourteen hours in the station, <u>the train</u> finally arrived.

As it is not 'the train' that has been waiting in the station for fourteen hours, this sentence also has to be rewritten:
> <u>After they had waited</u> fourteen hours in the station, the train finally arrived.

Read the following article. In it are several examples of pronouns being mixed up and of unattached phrases. Rewrite the article correcting these errors.

A Cure for the Common Cold?

Colds are everywhere; you cannot escape it. Having dosed yourself with every available remedy, the common cold still strikes. After centuries of observing symptoms, the common cold evades a cure.

Why should this be so? Having cured many more serious diseases, the common cold should be no problem. Hazarding an educated guess, the illness is too straightforward. Having very obvious symptoms, doctors cannot see the obvious solution. Diphtheria and TB are more complicated; doctors can cure it. But, faced with the uncomplicated nature of the common cold, the illness thrives. After centuries of sniffles and sore throats, doctors' surgeries are still full of people with colds.

Mother Nature still rules; it brings us the common cold. Having learnt to control many aspects of nature, the cold germ still flourishes.

DOUBLE NEGATIVES

Read the following dialogue:

TOM   He said he didn't want nothing.
DEBBIE What? He doesn't want nothing?
TOM   I couldn't hardly credit it.
DEBBIE He said he didn't know nothing about it.
TOM   About what? What didn't he know nothing about?
DEBBIE Nobody knows nothing, remember that, and nobody says nothing when the coppers come.

It is full of double negatives.

- **Double negatives** are grammatically **incorrect** because one is sufficient. In fact, the negative of a negative is a positive, so 'He doesn't want nothing' actually means 'He wants something'.

Activity 4

Rewrite the dialogue on the previous page removing all the double negatives.

LIKE AND AS

- '**Like**' is a **verb**, a **preposition** and an **adjective**, but it cannot perform the role of a conjunction:
    He said I am <u>like</u> my mother.
  'Like' in this sentence is a **preposition**.
    We have <u>like</u> tastes.
  In this sentence 'like' is an **adjective** describing tastes.

- In this sentence, however, 'like' has been used as a **conjunction**, which is **incorrect**:
    We did exactly <u>like</u> I wanted to.
  This should be rewritten as:
    We did exactly <u>as</u> I wanted to.

- '**As**' is the conjunction to use when you want to use a joining word meaning 'in the manner of' or 'in the same way that'.
Consider these examples:
  Incorrect: They said they wanted to sing exactly <u>like</u> I do.
  Correct: They said they wanted to sing exactly <u>as</u> I do.
  Correct: They said they wanted to sing exactly <u>like</u> me.

  Incorrect: <u>Like</u> I said at the time, it was the wrong thing to do.
  Correct: <u>As</u> I said at the time, it was the wrong thing to do.

Activity 5

Read the following letter. It is full of double negatives and mistaken uses of 'like'. Rewrite the letter correcting these errors.

Dear Joe,

I don't have nothing to say about what you mentioned in your last letter. It didn't come as no surprise to me, though. It hasn't nothing to do with me, that's all. Like I say, I haven't nothing to do with it.

But I must say I can't hardly accept your accusation. I have always treated you like a brother and now, like you've done a few times before, you don't give no credit for loyalty. There isn't nothing I can say then. If there isn't no trust between us, like I believe there isn't, then what's the point?

I hope there aren't no further accusations from your end. Like I say, there isn't nothing I wouldn't not do for you, but there has to be trust.

Yours sincerely,

Ben

SKILLCHECK   Check these statements to assess what you have learned from this section. If you cannot honestly tick every statement, go back over the section.

❑ I understand that I have to be careful about subject–verb agreements when the verb is next to a plural noun or after a compound subject.

❑ I can identify countable and uncountable nouns and know how to use them.

❑ I understand that it should always be clear to what or to whom a pronoun refers.

❑ I understand that phrases must refer to the subject of the clause that follows.

❑ I understand what double negatives are and how to avoid using them.

❑ I know when to use 'like' and when to use 'as'.

ANSWERS

Self-assessment questionnaire (page 5)

Nouns
1 Kate weather day holiday parents time hotel food beach week Rose
2 coach accident party pensioners motorway people observation junction outing seaside collision lorry cars fire passengers hatch driver injuries cause tragedy officer unit scene vehicle lane van
3 winning courage tenacity skill will hunger success honour

Verbs
1 want are willing to pay are can buy know doesn't worry do pride making makes think tell do write rate doesn't come think are don't buy go will show are do consider deserve (what)'s stopping
2 you are everybody wants hunting for employment takes time local employers have co-operated people who have been unemployed The services we provide include There are also skilled advisers Anybody over 18 who has been unemployed Each of the centres is situated Everybody is treated the same a friendly welcome is guaranteed Applications are not required Each of our centres is open Practical help and advice are at hand Good news is always welcome, so tell your friends

Sentences
1 *complete sentences* 1 3 7 13 16 17 18 *incomplete sentences* 2 4 5 6 8 9 10 11 12 14 15
2 My party our opponents Winning we voters prospects we taxes schools, hospitals, benefits and defence anyone money that the other lot we we advance we improvements we people they money I electorate party

Adjectives and adverbs
adjectives confident big Hollywood summer bulging bank American long school hungry new nation's Many youth Ageing pop teen young loveable popcorn-eating huge popular astute
adverbs Already anxiously enthusiastically cynically clearly eagerly literally accurately

Nouns (page 11)

Checkpoint A
group riot Guitars windows seats fans rampage night gig instruments singer way fans frenzy hall attendants venue spokesman repairs pounds

Checkpoint B
society equality fantasy equality goal freedom choice pursuit equality dream nation differences uniformity

Checkpoint C
Elvis Presley Tennessee United States Memphis Presley Heartbreak Hotel Blue Suede Shoes Hound Dog Love Me Tender Jailhouse Rock Elvis 'The King' Japan Elvis France Great Britain 'One-and-Only'

Checkpoint D
group swarm community gang

Checkpoint E
A ski resort a huge avalanche A fleet an unfortunate accident an hour's warning an unavoidable disaster An authoritative source an unqualified disaster

Checkpoint F
1 shoppers cornflakes and mueslis sameness product Tigercrunch ratio fibre eating AND enjoyment Breakfasts
2 Autographs signature statesmen money point secret Collectors auction-houses and dealers bucks Investors and speculators stars stars scarcity

Checkpoint G
visas passport German and English travellers cheques or sterling Visa, Access, Amex and Diners Club crystal, porcelain and liqueurs stamps stamps network and service

Checkpoint H
supporters   FA   authorities   players
spivs   followers

Pronouns (page 25)
Checkpoint A
me   They   We   they   I   them   you
I   them   I   I   you   me   you   I   you
Activity 1
I   You   I   I   it   it   They   us   They
or We   us or them   we or they   them
or us   You   them   you   us or me
We or I   We or I   We or I   her   him
you   it
Activity 2
Tony and me   Jackie and I   Jackie and
me   Jackie and I   Jackie and I   of me
Jackie and me   Jackie and I
Activities 3 and 4
3   yours   yours   mine or ours   ours
ours   theirs   mine   yours   ours
yours   ours   yours   ours
4   'The responsibility for this state of
affairs is mine,' said 'Hacker' Brown, the
team coach. 'The choice of players is
mine. I have my opinions, the board have
theirs. The players also have theirs. The
supporters have their moans about me, I
have mine about them.'
   'The trouble is he has his (ideas), the
supporters have theirs. They or the
supporters have their priorities, the club
has its.'
Activities 5 and 6
5   games which are threatening
parents and psychologists whose concern
big companies that or who just don't care
psychologists who are calling   smoking,
which results in ill-health   one expert who
asked   statement which he refused
6   a which   b that or which   c whose
d which   e whom   f which
Activity 7
Someone   Someone   Everything
Something   none   Someone
everything   Neither   Everyone
anyone   someone   Nothing   Everyone
Checkpoint B
What is the best way . . .?
Who knows . . .?   To whom can . . .?
Which is the best road. . . ?
Activity 8
yourself   ourselves   themselves   itself
yourself   myself

Verbs (page 38)
Checkpoint A
was   had taken   was   felt   gazed
loomed   is   cried   are doing   do
know   raised   howled   leapt   were
deceiving   could be   looked   saw
realised   was covered   could not be
knew   should be taking   was holding
was sensing   had been given   had
been   might reveal   do come   do have
asked   howled   reached
Activity 1
(suggested answers) Have   could   will
will have   should   may   will   have
need   will   could   might
can or will
Activity 2
My friend and I were having   I was
arguing   both the Empire and the Palace
in North Street were cinemas   My friend
insists   the Empire was a theatre   Every
one of my friends likes reading   We
especially like   The sports page, the local
news, the fashion articles and the
crossword puzzle also please us   You
and your reporters have to keep up
Checkpoint B
present infinitives   to tell   to be   to do
to marry   to wait   To marry   to repent
to marry   to learn   To err   to forgive
past infinitives   To have done   To have
done   To have waited
Checkpoint C
active verbs   has revealed   prefer
were   has indicated   express   prefer
have   kept   do not surprise   said   do
not bite   are   do not make   *passive
verbs*   was considered   was
commissioned   was conducted   was
discovered   were named   were disliked
infinitive form   to be
Activity 3
a Every penny of their wages was earned
by the workers.   b The experiment was
conducted by the scientist under strictly
controlled conditions.
c The lawn was cut by the gardener with
the new mower.   d The defendant was
found guilty as charged by the judge.
e The customer was phoned by the
secretary with an apology.
Activity 4
The time was midnight. The city was quiet
and all the bad guys were home in bed.

Somewhere a lonely trumpet player was playing a sad tune. It was quiet, too quiet. Suddenly, the sound of a bullet shattered the peace. Car tyres screeched in the darkness. A body fell to the pavement. It seemed that, after all, not all the bad guys were asleep. Mickey Chandler, private eye, was instantly awake. He could smell trouble a mile away. He reached out for his automatic and crossed to the window. He scanned the empty streets. Out there, there were bad guys to defeat. He was the man for the task. No criminal was safe when Chandler was in the city.

Checkpoint D
present participles Thinking holidaying Disappointing (used as an adjective) surprising (adjective) Reeling Considering Watching
past participles Bored carried Tired led thrown thwarted (adjective) fleeced (adjective)

Checkpoint E
1 putting feeling dreading complaining choosing loving letting bringing
2 Their their Your their

Adjectives (page 52)
Checkpoint A
Violent Pitch Premier League excited angry Several unruly playing Astonished unhappy absolute flabbergasted sick Butterworth million-pound Out-of-control bitter disenchanted Baykop second visiting this disgraceful unacceptable anonymous serious football match next

Checkpoint B
quality Dear wonderful old summer distant important crucial lousy possible spanking new leisure multiplex *quantity* many four no much *possessive* their your my Our *demonstrative* This these *interrogative* What *others* every All no Any

Activity 3
It's the only shoe to choose It's a combination of colour on its sole It's a matter of taste if it's not good taste its own distinctive style its own indefinable quality it's always going to be Bond it's a matter

Activity 4
most boring worse more exciting better cheaper slimmer least more attractive richer wealthiest daftest happiest more more interesting funniest more stupid

Adverbs (page 61)
Checkpoint A
emotionally frankly yesterday suddenly Truthfully quite too successfully badly deeply completely very ruthlessly directly alarmingly straight exceedingly persuasively terribly always totally professionally proudly utterly equally

Checkpoint B
manner Slowly certainly intently sadly cruelly monotonously closely magnetically surprisingly Staggeringly malevolently alarmingly heavily Suddenly *time* Daily Soon Now Now *place* Out over everywhere *degree* very much (bigger) really too utterly *interrogative* Why how What *emphasis, doubt and negation* Unfortunately (was)n't Perhaps maybe Surely Undoubtedly Indeed Surely (was)n't

Activity 3
(suggested answers) a She was more desperate to succeed than the other girl. She was the most desperate of all to succeed. b He dressed more elegantly and tastefully than his brother. Of all the brothers, he dressed the most elegantly and tastefully. c The game gave less in the way of opportunity for him to shine than the previous fixture. Of all the games, this one gave him the least opportunity to shine. d The tenor sang worse on that particular occasion than on the previous one. On that particular occasion, the tenor sang the worst he had every sung. e I feel better than I thought, considering what I've been through. I feel the best I could expect to feel considering what I've been through.

Prepositions (page 67)
Checkpoint A
in outside of of in with of for in of with through beneath On in by of in of In at

outside   by (a yob)   to   In   of   in
of   for   at   on   for

Activity 1
in   for   of   to   in   Without   by/to
At   of   on   to   above   about

Activity 2
about it   talking about   warming of the
planet   in a very serious condition   in a
position   backed by   in the world
listen to them   Most of them   round the
bend   the courage of your ignorance
about this earth   you live on   On your
bike   Get off your hobby horse   Having
a conversation with you   next to
impossible

Activity 3
from you and me   any difference to her
really was from us   It was for them
wasn't appreciated by them   done to you
and me   can't see past him   Between
you and me   trying to tell us   friends
with you and me   up to her

Conjunctions and interjections (page 72)
Checkpoint A
AND   and   or   or   or   but   until
after   before   when

Activities 1 and 2
(The answers to these two exercises are
suggestions. Other variations may also be
correct.)
1   It gives us great pleasure to write to
inform you of some good news, which is
that you have won a prize in our lottery.
Because you are a valued customer, your
name was entered into our draw last
month. The lucky numbers were chosen
and you are one of the fortunate prize-
winners. If you want to receive this
valuable prize, you must take these steps.
Send in three thousand packet tops of our
cereal 'Teethcracker' and we will send you
the cash prize.
     This offer remains open until June 25th
of this year, so if we do not hear from you
by then, the cash prize will be forfeit.
2   It had come from another world by
travelling through space in a spacecraft,
which could go faster than the speed of
light.
     Its masters had realised that the alien
would be conspicuous in Dorking High
Street. Because the bug eyes, the 24 feet

and the light that flashed on top of its
head would attract attention, they had
devised an instant camouflage. The only
problem was that the disguise chosen
looked just like the Prime Minister!
     As it walked down Dorking High Street,
people stared at it. When the humans
came up to it, they seized its hand and it
wondered why. Although it had been
instructed how to deal with some
eventualities, this was different. Only five
minutes after landing earth people were
asking for its autograph. They seemed to
know it.

Activity 3
(suggested answers)   Well, I never!
Hey, what are you going on about now?
Well, you could have knocked me down
with a feather!   What!   Well, I never
thought that would happen!   What a
shock!   What a shame!   Nonsense!
Of course, the world's gone mad these
days!   Rubbish! Of course it is!

More about sentences (page 79)

Checkpoint A
complete sentences   Usually, it's not done
to be in the red   But when the red is the
laser red of the Gaudy Élite 80, then who
wouldn't be in the red?   And the
performance isn't that bad either.   It's
touches like these that make driving
pleasurable.   Get in the red.   Your bank
manager won't even mind.
incomplete sentences   In the red   Hardly
anyone.   An electric twenty-first century
red.   A stylish, sensual red.   Not your
ordinary red of a football shirt.   But the
red of an élite.   A Gaudy Élite.   Top
speed of 125 m.p.h.   Power-assisted
steering.   Sun-roof.   Automatic gears.
But she will notice.

Checkpoint B
type 1 The bank was in the middle of the
High Street.   There was the usual quota
of loungers.   It was not particularly busy
inside the bank.   There were a few
people waiting for the tellers.   Then it
was their turn.   These were bank
robbers.
type 2 The getaway car glided to a halt
near it.   Shoppers went about their

business.   The two men in the back seat got out of the car.   They looked around. The queue shortened.
type 3   No one paid any attention to the nondescript vehicle.   The driver left the engine running.   Then they walked the few yards to the door of the bank.   The men joined a short queue.   Suddenly, the men pulled stockings out of their pockets. They pulled them over their faces.   Now they were brandishing guns.   They issued instructions rapidly and gruffly.
type 4   Everything appeared normal. The men seemed to be without a care in the world.   They seemed to be waiting patiently for their turn.

Checkpoint C
simple   The popularity of television soap operas never seems to wane.   The fascination of soaps has to do with familiarity.   For many people, these soap characters are real people.
compound   'Coronation Street', 'EastEnders' and 'Brookside' have been running for years now and audiences in their millions continue to watch them. Most soap actors are totally identified with their characters and are scarcely known by their own names.   Some actors do not mind this, but others resent it.   Viewers regularly send letters to 'Emmerdale' or write to 'EastEnders' characters with advice.   Perhaps these fanatics lack something in their own lives, or want to lose themselves in a fictional world.   The characters of the soaps are only imitation people, but try telling that to the millions of fans.
multiple   Audiences identify with the characters, make them their 'friends' and live their lives with them.   They enjoy the fame, they have the security of a long-running series, but they lose their identity to their fictional character. Escapism is an integral part of soap operas, but it can be dangerous and people can avoid facing up to their own problems.

Activity 3
(suggested answers)   a When she lost her purse, she reported it to the police.   b The father cooked the meal and called the children to the table, but they did not come.   c Although the DJ played the song and repeated it by general request, he refused to play it a third time.   d As the car picked up speed it passed the slow-moving lorry.   e He tried to study, found it boring, so packed it in.

   Checkpoint D
pour some of it into the teapot   put one teaspoon of tea in the pot for each person   Pour the boiling water into the pot   The tea should infuse for at least five minutes

Checkpoint E
which it is difficult to match   which has only been in existence for a few years where business people from all over the world converge   that has few equals whose population has been through good times and bad times   when the Czech wine flows and Czech fine cuisine flourishes

Checkpoint F
time   when we review the school year When exam time comes around again When the time comes to make a decision   *place*   Where we haven't been doing so well   where it is convenient for staff and pupils   *reason* because all of us want to do well as naturally it is an important phase Because we will have prepared well   as this is clearly a very important matter for the school

Checkpoint G
manner   how good I feel about passing my test   *comparison or degree*   than I have done   just as much as I do   *result* so I was prepared to be disappointed *purpose*   so I can give you some tips In order that we can catch up with things so that it's convenient for us both *condition*   If you have any doubts yourself about taking the test   *concession* Although I started learning to drive with great hopes of success   though please try to ring me

Checkpoint H
that council charges will have to be increased significantly from April next year What has not yet been decided   That it will be substantial   that this government is not interested in providing decent local services   that funds previously provided to subsidise local services   what the government is up to   that our voice has been ignored   what lies in store   what central government has instigated

Common grammatical errors
(page 95)

Activity 1
A huge range of personal CD players *is* available Round every street corner *exist* enticing ads *Haven't* you all enough problems? But you and your mates *love* your music. The choice and solution *are* easy. Across the globe more Boni CD players *are* bought than any other brand. You and Boni *possess* the secret.

Activity 2
Much has been made of the many difficulties of learning to be computer literate, but there are fewer problems than many people claim. It is true that many difficulties have to be put up with in the many initial attempts to master a computer, but many fewer than usually predicted. Fewer people than you would expect have much trouble with learning this important new skill.

Activity 3
Colds are everywhere; you cannot escape them. Although you may have dosed yourself with every available remedy, the common cold still strikes. The common cold evades a cure, after centuries of observation of its symptoms. Why should this be so? As many more serious diseases have been cured, the common cold should be no problem. To hazard an educated guess, perhaps the illness is just too straightforward. Although it has very obvious symptoms, doctors cannot see the obvious solution. Diphtheria and TB are more complicated; doctors can cure them. But, when they are faced with the uncomplicated nature of the common cold, the illness thrives. After centuries of sniffles and sore throats, doctors' surgeries are still full of people with colds.

Mother Nature still rules; she brings us the common cold. Although we have learnt to control many aspects of nature, the cold germ still flourishes.

Activity 4
MAN He said he didn't want anything.
WOMAN What? He doesn't want anything?
MAN I could hardly credit it.
WOMAN He said he *didn't know anything/knew nothing* about it.
MAN About what? What *didn't he know anything/did he know nothing* about?

WOMAN Nobody knows anything, remember that, and nobody says anything when the coppers come.

Activity 5
I *don't have anything/have nothing* to say about what you mentioned in your last letter. It *didn't come as any/came as no* surprise to me, though. It *hasn't anything/has nothing* to do with me, that's all. As I say, I *haven't anything/have nothing* to do with it. But I must say I can hardly accept your accusation. I have always treated you like a brother and now, as you've done a few times before, you *don't give any/give no* credit for loyalty. There *isn't anything/is nothing* I can say then. If there *isn't any/is no* trust between us, as I believe there isn't, then what's the point? I hope there *aren't any/are no* further accusations from your end. As I say, there *isn't anything/is nothing* I wouldn't do for you, but there has to be trust.

ANSWERS